The authors have given us a stimulating and informative treatment of a long-neglected subject—the grounding of Methodist polity and practice in a well-articulated theology. Both of these have been placed in their historical setting, but a convincing rationale is provided for their continued use today. This book will be a great resource for the training of United Methodist clergy and laity.

H. Paul Smith
The Florida Methodist Foundation

The history of United Methodism has been a struggle to make its theology an authentic expression of the Christian gospel and to make its polity an authentic expression of its theology. The understanding of these complex developments is only now emerging, but this emergence is of critical importance for United Methodist self-understanding. Wilson and Harper are exploring this arena and helping to enrich our self-knowledge. This study points in the direction we must take to interpret our past and plan our future.

Dr. Thomas A. Langford
The Divinity School
Duke University

United Methodism has needed such a book for at least a generation, but never more than now. The greater integration of our beliefs and our polity, as well as greater clarity of the two, are indispensable steppingstones toward the renaissance that is to come.

Dr. George E. Hunter III
E. Stanley Jones School
of World Mission and Evangelism
Asbury Theological Seminary

This is a significant book and one which should be read widely in the United Methodist Church and used in theological schools requiring a course in United Methodist polity. It will also be useful to pastors and laypersons who want to be more informed on the subject. The authors are to be commended for the insights they have brought to the subject. This book fills a real need.

Alan K. Waltz
The General Board of Discipleship
of the United Methodist Church

FAITH
A • N • D
FORM

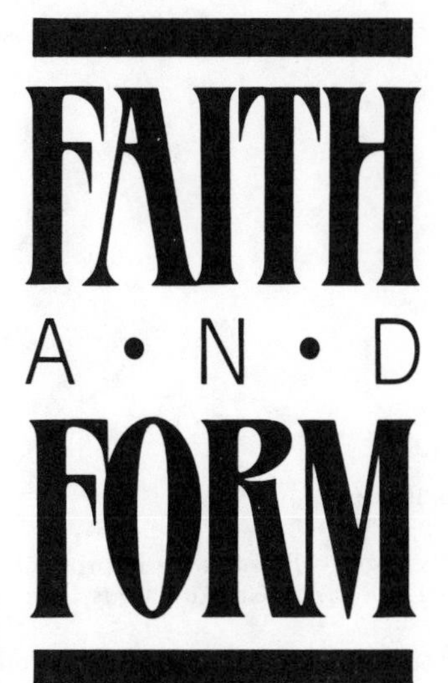

FAITH AND FORM

A UNITY OF THEOLOGY & POLITY IN THE UNITED METHODIST TRADITION

ROBERT L. WILSON
STEVE HARPER

FRANCIS ASBURY PRESS
of Zondervan Publishing House
Grand Rapids, Michigan

FAITH AND FORM

The Francis Asbury Press is an imprint of Zondervan Publishing House,
1415 Lake Drive S.E., Grand Rapids, Michigan, 49506.

Library of Congress Cataloging in Publication Data

Wilson, Robert Leroy, 1925–
Faith and form: a unity of theology and polity in the United Methodist tradition / Robert L. Wilson, Steve Harper.
p. cm.
Bibliography: p.
Includes index.
ISBN 0-310-51521-1
1. United Methodist Church (U.S.)—Doctrines. 2. United Methodist Church (U.S.)—Government. 3. Methodist Church—Doctrines. 4. Methodist Church—Government. I. Harper, Steve. II. Title.
BX8382.2.Z5W54 1988
287'.6—dc19 88–452
CIP

Edited by James E. Ruark
Designed by Louise Bauer

Printed in the United States of America

89 90 91 92 93 / CH / 10 9 8 7 6 5 4 3 2

Contents

Preface

This is a book about how the beliefs of United Methodist people shape the way they organize the church. In making this presentation we believe we are consistent with John Wesley's concern to join knowledge and vital piety. And we believe we are consistent with those contemporary Wesleyan scholars who are rediscovering Wesley's emphasis on practical divinity.

It is inconceivable that Wesley would have consciously separated theology and polity in original Methodism. On the contrary, the way he ordered the movement is a direct reflection of his theology, especially the order of salvation. Every facet of original Methodist structure has a connection with theological content. And it is precisely this interplay between theology and polity that makes Methodism pulsate with life.

We have written this book to make a fresh witness to the necessity of interplay between theology and polity in United Methodism. Unfortunately, we believe, the last fifty to one hundred years give evidence of a separation of these two elements, and both a theological and structural weakening as a result. We hope that this book will make a positive contribution to the rejoining of the two.

Theology does not exist in a vacuum. Beliefs that people

hold inevitably influence the social and cultural setting and in turn are influenced by them. Polity is also affected by shifts in theological emphases and by the responses the church makes to its continually changing social and cultural context.

Consequently, this book is about how theology and polity interact in United Methodism. The first section focuses on traditional, well-established beliefs in the church. We have made no attempt to be novel in this section, but rather we seek to present the major, basic tenets of our theology that have been recognized by the vast majority of United Methodists as being at the heart of our tradition.

The second section focuses on the way United Methodism orders the church. Here, too, the emphasis is on what might be called "Methodism at its best." We do not apologize for presenting what ought to be, along with descriptions of what is. The third section of the book examines issues of faith and practice that the denomination must deal with as it moves into its third century.

It is important to note that this book was originally conceived as a text for seminarians and/or pastors. This largely accounts for its foundational nature. In that light it serves as a companion volume to the *Book of Discipline*, the *Works* of Wesley, and other normative texts in the Wesleyan tradition. The notes have been designed to provide numerous points where further investigation can take place. We have provided a list of readings at the end of the book that can facilitate further study.

The authors are indebted to many persons for their assistance, critical reading of the manuscript, and encouragement while this book took its final form. A special thanks is due Candice Y. Sloan of the J. M. Ormond Center for assisting with the research and the preparation of the manuscript. It is hoped that this book will enable United Methodists both to understand their church better and to witness and minister more effectively in it.

Robert L. Wilson
Steve Harper

PART I

WHAT UNITED METHODISTS BELIEVE

Chapter 1

The Theological Heritage

To speak of the theological heritage of United Methodism is to speak in the plural, not the singular. It would be difficult to find another denomination whose theology is shaped and influenced by so many streams of tradition. To speak of our theological heritage is to speak of something like the Mississippi River: it is an identifiable body, but it owes its existence to major and minor tributaries. Our theological heritage can be identified, but only with reference to its pre-Wesley, Wesley, and post-Wesley tributaries.

This chapter will explore some of the major tributaries of this theological heritage. The purpose will be to show how contemporary United Methodism stands within the larger Christian community, and how the denomination is the benefactor of important elements from other traditions. The focus will be on ecumenicity and enrichment. In a subsequent chapter we will give attention to certain doctrinal distinctives in our theological heritage. For now, the goal will be to show how persons in other centuries and communions have influenced the development of the Methodist theological tradition. Admittedly, this exploration will be far from comprehensive. But one hopes it will be accurate and descriptive enough for us to sense our indebtedness to and connection with the whole church of Jesus Christ.

PRE-WESLEY INFLUENCES

John Wesley consciously grounded Methodism's theological heritage in what was called "primitive Christianity."[1] Wesley believed that the theology and polity of early church history contained a richness and normativeness that God had raised for Methodism to emphasize and perpetuate.

Wesley's indebtedness to the early church is obvious and extensive. From Augustine in the Western Church he was enriched in his theology of sin. In the Eastern Church the Cappadocians greatly helped him develop a theology of Christian perfection that included a view of Christianity as a faith pilgrimage. Additionally, in his writings Wesley bore witness to the influence of others like Clement of Rome, Ignatius, Polycarp, Justin Martyr, Irenaeus, Origen, Clement of Alexandria, Cyprian, Macarius, and Ephraem Syrus. He did not accept them as perfect representatives or exponents of Christian theology, but on the whole he accepted their writings "because they describe true, genuine Christianity, and direct us to the strongest evidence of Christian doctrine."[2]

Moving beyond the early church, the influence of the Reformers can be noted, especially in the doctrine of justification by faith. The mystics must also be included, particularly their emphasis on Christlikeness.[3] Closer to Wesley's own time, it is possible to see influences in post-Tridentine Roman Catholicism, subsequent developments in Eastern Orthodoxy, Pietism, Evangelicals and Independents, and even the Quakers. The result is a remarkable eclecticism that made Methodism richer than it could have possibly become through any single influence.[4]

However, such eclecticism had to have a vehicle of expression, some identity with a recognized church. For Wesley, this vehicle was Anglicanism—the second major tradition to influence our theological heritage.

Anglicanism

All his life John Wesley was "a Church of England man."[5] Its influence can be especially noted through the *Book of Common Prayer,* the *Homilies,* the Articles of Religion, the means of grace, and church order. Because the connection with Anglicanism is so close, each of these merits further attention.

Apart from the Bible, no single book influenced Wesley as much as the *Book of Common Prayer.* Through daily use of it, he was shaped in the fundamentals of his theology, the essence of his spirituality, the heart of his worship, and the matrix of his polity. The *Book of Common Prayer* was the tangible integration of theology and polity, not only for Anglicanism, but for Wesley himself. It is not surprising that he abridged the Order for Morning Prayer and offered it to the soon-to-be American Methodist Episcopal Church for their Sunday Service.[6]

The *Homilies* also provided theological influence, especially those that related to salvation, faith, and good works.[7] These *Homilies* expressed the heart of Wesley's theology—soteriology—and from them he received a basic substance and structure to communicate. The substance was a theology of grace. The structure was an "order of salvation" that related both to traditional theology and to practical divinity, especially Wesley's primary nurturing bodies: societies, classes, and bands. It is important to remember that Wesley used these *Homilies* during the turbulent days of April and May 1738 as he struggled to accept the truth of the Moravian emphasis on the instantaneous conversion. What he found in the *Homilies* (together with the Bible and the witness of faithful Christians) served to prepare him for his Aldersgate experience. And as Methodism emerged as a movement on its own, it is very likely that the *Homilies* influenced his decision in 1746 to use "standard sermons" as the model for theological content and expression.[8]

The Thirty-nine Articles of Religion of the Anglican Church was Wesley's theological confession. He did not accept every article, line, and term, as his revision and reduction of the thirty-nine articles to twenty-four for American Methodists make clear. The Anglican Articles were more Calvinistic than Wesley wanted the new American church to be. But on the home front in England, he never found the Articles bothersome enough to engage in a revision for British Methodism. The Articles of Religion were a faithful expression of the creeds (Apostles, Nicean, Athanasian, and Chalcedonian) and as such were influential in our theological heritage.

The means of grace were acts of devotion that the Anglican and other churches recognized as the normal channels used by God to convey grace to people. Wesley named five as Instituted: Prayer, Searching the Scriptures, the Lord's Supper, Fasting, and Christian Conference. He named three as Prudential: Avoiding Harm, Doing Good, and Attending the Ordinances of God.[9] Through his preaching of sermons like "The Means of Grace" and in the "General Rules of the United Societies," Wesley emphasized the centrality of the means of grace in Methodist formation. As such, they became a point of synthesis between theology and polity in early Methodism. They were one of Wesley's best attempts to actualize his commitment to rejoin in Methodism those two elements in Christianity so long divided: knowledge and vital piety. And they stand as his best expression of the use of experience in doing theology.

Finally, one can see the influence of Anglicanism in Wesley's lifelong concern for authority, order, and connection in Methodism. By 1743, Methodism was sufficiently dispersed and diverse to warrant some attempts at structural unity. Wesley's first official attempt came in the 1743 publication of the "General Rules of the United Societies." A year later, he called the first "annual conference" that brought preachers together, not unlike Convocation in the Anglican Church, to pray and talk about what to teach, how to teach, and what to do.[10] The annual conference became the backbone of the Methodist movement and remains so today. In these ways and more, the influence of Anglicanism was profound and extensive.

Puritanism

With such a close and significant connection to Anglicanism, one might be tempted to overlook a third major stream of pre-Wesley influence, namely, Puritanism.[11] Literally running through Wesley's veins was the blood of parents and ancestors who were Puritans and who saw allegiance to God as a higher duty than adherence to a particular church. Ironically, both Anglicanism and Puritanism were expressions of Christians coming out from parent churches. But by the eighteenth century, the spirit of independence was better represented in the Puritan movement than in institutional Anglicanism. Unfortunately this independence has been misinterpreted to mean that Wesley and the early Methodists were mavericks and malcontents. More accurately, they were persons of courage and conviction. They were persons of conscience, a trait that harkens back to the importance of conscience as a hallmark of the Puritan tradition.[12]

It is important to note that personal conviction was tempered by one's participation in the church or faith community. Puritanism did not advocate privatized or isolated experiences. But at the same time it allowed liberty to look at the church and theology critically. In this respect the Puritans more nearly represented the Reformation spirit, and this spirit found its way into early Methodism.

The Puritans also provided a strong sense of covenant. Wesley's theology of covenant and the Covenant Service itself can both be linked to Puritan sources. Furthermore, his decision to add "experience" to the Anglican trilateral of

"Scripture, tradition, and reason" is at least partly due to the influence of Puritanism. The doctrines of justification, assurance, sanctification, sin in believers, and final justification were all enriched by Puritan teaching. A concern for practical divinity was fueled by the Puritan emphasis on the individual, family, church, and world. And finally, Wesley's *Christian Library* (1749–1755) includes more Puritans than any other category of authors—almost 44 percent in all.

This brief survey of pre-Wesley influences reveals our deep connection with and indebtedness to historic Christianity. It is clear that Wesley was on a quest for truth and life, and he knew that he could find something positive in virtually every expression of the Christian faith. This ecumenical spirit runs deep in our theological heritage, and it has its origins in the earliest expressions of Methodism.

Implications of This Influence

Two implications flow from all this. First, Wesley was not a "fundamentalist" if by that we mean a person who is seeking the reduction of truth to its fewest possible expressions. On the contrary, he was looking for truth in its broadest and largest expressions. Second, Wesley's use of historic Christianity was not subjective or inconsistent. He was able to use a variety of traditions because he had an organizing principle—a filter through which to screen the traditions in order to mine the gold that was there. Primitive Christianity was that filter, as reflected in the creeds and in the subsequent confessions that expanded and interpreted them.[13]

These two features prevented early Methodism from falling off on the one side of myopic legalism or on the other side of doctrinal indifferentism. They enable us to claim one of the richest theological heritages of any denomination. They also helped specifically to shape polity in terms of such things as the ordering and appointment of ministers, the conduct of worship, the administration of the sacraments, the nurture of believers, and the maintaining of order.

INFLUENCES OF WESLEY'S CONTEMPORARIES

John Wesley and early Methodism were also influenced by eighteenth-century events, persons, and movements. Although Methodism was neither defined nor captured by the eighteenth century, it was certainly part of it. And our theological heritage is influenced by the century in which Methodism was born.

First, the eighteenth century was a time when the national base of England was shifting from agriculture to industry, from rural to urban, from divine right to a new regard for the individual. The Enlightenment was affecting England philosophically, scientifically, politically, economically, sociologically, and religiously.[14] And as with any period of rapid, radical social change, people were falling through the cracks. England was struggling with problems of overpopulation in the cities, crime, alcoholism, unemployment, child labor abuse, and more. New groups of oppressed people emerged as the gap between the upper and lower classes widened.

These social dynamics were highly influential in Wesley's decision to be a "folk theologian" and to make Methodism a movement of the common people. English society also sheds light on why Wesley resolutely maintained the connection between personal and social holiness. God laid the forgotten people on his heart, and Methodism's theology and polity reflect this even now. Wesley believed the church was supposed to be the nation's conscience, and he always believed God had raised up Methodism to reform English society.

Second, the eighteenth century was a time of intellectual revolution. The Enlightenment had expanded the world, and with it the world of ideas. Travel, trade, and advances in almost every field created a new optimism and respect for human potential. People viewed themselves less as part of some divine, hierarchical system than as free thinkers in their own right. Concepts of "truth" and "freedom" were enlarged and relativized in comparison with previous centuries in England. Reason was exalted.

By temperament and training, Wesley reflected the age. During his childhood, his parents noted his preference for reason and logic. At the university he became a skilled debater. Like many of his Anglican contemporaries, he wanted a "reasonable faith," yet he was unwilling to take this as far as many did. He refused to embrace or advocate "speculative latitudinarianism."[15] Methodism exhibited a balance between revelation and reason that society and churches (liberal and conservative) in general were unable to strike.

Third, the eighteenth century was a time of ecclesiastical stagnation. At the beginning of the seventeenth century, Anglicanism had remarkable power and influence. A century later that had been sharply reduced. Established Anglicanism was largely a maintainer of the status quo and a reflection of the gap in society between the rich and the poor. Even its commitment to a *via media* (middle way) in the theology was something of an attempt to hold varying theologies with minimal controversy.

At this point early Methodism felt its greatest pressure. Wesley struggled for more than fifty years to be in the church but not of it. He continually defended himself against charges that he was not a true Church of England man.[16] In retrospect we can see that this tension is what made him more of a reformer than an institutionalist. But he went right on resolutely maintaining that Methodism was nothing more than an expression of *true* Anglicanism.

All this is to say that theology and polity never exist in a vacuum. They are not developed *ex nihilo*. Rather, they are created and expressed in relation to the culture and the times. Wesley benefited from previous centuries, but he had to live in his own. He ordered the message and structures of Methodism to express scriptural Christianity in ways that would make a difference to his age.

We must not underestimate the genius of Methodism's living in the eighteenth century largely without being co-opted by it. From an institutional perspective it is extremely difficult to exist as an alternative to society. The tendency is to embrace society's values and mores in order to be accepted and to prosper. That Wesley offered the eighteenth century a distinctive alternative in terms of theology and polity is significant, and it is part of the spirit that makes up our heritage.

The Role of Family and the Holy Living Tradition

Wesley's ability to guide Methodism as a distinctive alternative was not automatic or accidental. It was the result of two other primary eighteenth-century influences that operated in his life. We begin with his parents, Samuel and Susanna. The atmosphere and activities of the home influenced Wesley for the rest of his life. Both Samuel and Susanna were living expressions of a rare combination of Puritan sentiments and Anglican loyalties.

Samuel provided a clear love of Scripture, a regular use of the *Book of Common Prayer,* a facility with verse and hymnody, a commitment to personal devotion, a use of the means of grace, and a vision for world mission. Susanna reflected these same concerns and added to them a love of reading, a commitment to self-examination and diary keeping, the now-famous educational/devotional method of training her children, her leadership of the Epworth society, and her weekly, personal attention to each of the children. Unfortunately Wesley never had this kind of home as an adult, but the importance of parental influence can be seen in many of his personal and corporate practices.

However, it was Wesley's decision to align himself with the "holy living" tradition in the eighteenth century that most profoundly shaped his theology and polity. It was the holy living tradition that introduced him to primitive Christianity and the life of discipline and virtue that reflected it. The idea of human perfectability, not as a philosophical concept but as one's practical participation with God in Christ, came to be Wesley's primary motivation.[17] In its essence it meant the offering up of one's whole life to God as a living sacrifice, loving God and neighbor as completely as possible, and experiencing the renewal of the *imago dei* in our humanity.

The holy living tradition provided Wesley with his view of theology as an "order of salvation"—a pilgrimage in response to prevenient, justifying, sanctifying, and glorifying grace. It enabled Wesley to see the union of personal and social holiness in ways others had not. And it gave him his basic understanding of Christianity as faith working by love unto holiness.[18] In short, the holy living tradition provided the means of receiving, interpreting, and integrating the theological dynamics of the pre-Wesley influences.

It also provided early Methodism with its basic structural features. The societies that came out of this part of the tradition were operating in a variety of ways in England and occasionally in the Church of England. The Holy Club at Oxford, Wesley's group ministry in Georgia, and his connection with the Moravians are all connected with the general current of holy living that was flowing in the eighteenth century. As with everything else, Wesley did not embrace every facet of the holy living tradition (e.g., extreme mysticism, tendencies toward legalism, and quietism), but he did take the best of the tradition and consciously sought to make Methodism a representative of it.

The influences of the eighteenth century served both as a funnel to catch historic Christianity and as a milieu in which early Methodism developed. These served to transfer our heritage of breadth and balance through the eighteenth century into the nineteenth. A study of the eighteenth century reveals a providential series of choices that gave Methodism its basic substance and form. A study of early Methodism (and its formative sources) may well serve us today as we move into our third century.

POST-WESLEY INFLUENCES

With the establishment of American Methodism as an independent denomination in 1784, the scene shifts from

England to the New World. And by all accounts, the ensuing two hundred years are difficult to describe. The issue is complicated by a virtual explosion of *theologies* within Methodism, a series of splits and unions, and finally the addition of the Evangelical United Brethren heritage. The result is a theological proliferation and complexity that only recently has begun to be studied.

Robert Chiles made the first serious attempt by roughly dividing theological development into three periods, each with a representative theologian: Orthodoxy (Richard Watson), Ethical Arminianism (John Miley), and Personal Idealism (Albert Knudson).[19] His study remains substantive and helpful, but it is dated in that it concluded with the year 1935.

Thomas A. Langford has provided an excellent analysis that updates our theological heritage and also expands the list of significant theologians.[20] His approach shows the difficulty in limiting the influences to a few categories. Instead, it speaks for a closer examination of individual theologians in America and Great Britain if we are to assess our theological heritage accurately. For him, this is especially important because a number of major Methodist theologians are still alive and exerting continuing influence on the denomination.

Finally, Albert Outler has proposed yet another model for studying post-Wesley influences.[21] He suggests a three-phased development that is not so historically or biographically oriented as it is thematically defined. Furthermore, Outler emphasizes that no phase can be limited to a certain period in American Methodism; rather, the phases are more like layers or types of study that have been noted. Phase 1 focuses on Wesley the man and Methodism the movement. Its emphases are biographical and internal. Studies in this phase have sometimes lacked objectivity, making Wesley more of a hero and Methodism more of a pure faith expression than either deserve.

Phase 2 focuses on a particular aspect of Wesley and/or Methodism and seeks to relate that aspect to the larger Christian community. Our theological heritage is developed in a way that stresses ecumenicity and relevance to specific issues in church and society. In this phase one must struggle with the temptation to lose the real Wesley or Methodism by making a part appear to be the whole.

Outler then offers a phase 3 for Wesleyan studies that focuses on Wesley's works, his sources, and Methodism's formative documents. This phase holds the promise of offering the whole Wesley and Methodism while at the same time keeping our place in the larger church clearly in mind.

Besides these analyses, we must note the contributions of the Evangelical United Brethren tradition, which ran alongside Methodism for two hundred years and which actually preceded Methodism in coming to America.[22] The lives of Jacob Albright, Philip Otterbein, and Martin Boehm each merit more study, as well as the churches they began. In terms of early American Methodism, there is need for further study with respect to Thomas Coke and especially Francis Asbury. All this is to say that there is still much work to be done in seeing the post-Wesley influences with the same kind of summarization and synthesis that are possible in previous periods.

The Present State of Affairs

A general assessment of this period reveals some insights and raises some questions that affect the present state of affairs in United Methodism. First, we note the lingering but diminishing influence of Wesley as an authority for Methodist theology. The first century of American Methodism shows a dominance of what we might call "Methodist orthodoxy." This was largely due to the Course of Study, a program of required readings and examinations for prospective clergy. However, early American Methodism never embraced Wesley as an authority the way British Methodism did. By 1825 there were already theologians who felt at liberty to "interpret" Wesley and produce theology in a way unknown in early Methodism. By the end of the nineteenth century, this tendency was firmly established as the dominant approach in the denomination. It was this trend that in the 1930s caused

George Croft Cell to speak of the loss and recovery of Wesley in American Methodism.[23]

The years since Cell's work was published have by no means clarified Wesley's authority and influence in the denomination. However, a new generation of Wesley scholars and the commitment of Abingdon Press to publish the bicentennial edition of Wesley's *Works* are signs that he is being given serious attention. The time is right for a careful reassessment of Wesley's role in contemporary United Methodism.

Second, we can note a concerted effort to place Methodism in the larger Christian community and the world. The past hundred years have been especially noteworthy in this regard as Methodist theologians have entered into dialogue with other Christian churches and have been at the forefront of missional endeavors. This is especially noteworthy at the point of interfaith dialogues, quests for denominational union, social impact, and Christian missions. These ventures have sometimes been criticized as giving up too much for the sake of unity or mission, but they have prevented Methodism from turning inward.

Third, post-Wesley influences have shaped a formidable theology of grace, centering in the person and work of Christ and finding expression in a variety of human experiences and responses. This dimension varies from clearly orthodox expressions to heterodox ones. But in it all, United Methodism has sought a theology that portrays the divine-human encounter in a way that preserves God's sovereignty and human freedom. At its best, United Methodism has produced a heritage of liberty without license, experience without subjectivism, and content without legalism.

Fourth, we can note a drift from historic orthodoxy toward a more independent, free-lance spirit in theologizing. American Methodist theologians were influenced by European contemporaries. Everyone was influenced by the empirical spirit that provided a rationale for using theology to probe, question, and even deny historic tenets of Christianity. The result has been a corpus of theology less intentionally connected to classical Christianity than was true in previous centuries.[24]

This fact has resulted in something of a separation between theology and polity. Institutional Methodism has had to protect itself from perceived radical attempts (both liberal and conservative) to alter the shape of the church. Thus the polity of the church has remained fairly constant while theological emphases have varied widely. Perhaps the clearest example of this came in the late 1960s when certain theologians declared that "God is dead," which by implication called the existence of the church into serious question. Paul Stookey of the singing group Peter, Paul and Mary even wrote a hit song during this time that told of a preacher who said, "God is dead, but the church will go on living."

The past thirty years have seen a widening gap between the church and the seminaries. The result is a degree of theological malaise that was recognized by the 1984 General Conference's establishment of task forces to study the doctrinal statement, the theology of ministry, and the theology of mission. Happily, there are signs that this separatist trend is reversing itself. United Methodist seminaries are more openly acknowledging their service and accountability to the denomination, and even to a more classical understanding of the Christian faith. A closer connection between seminary and church will strengthen our future theological development and its relationship to polity.

Fifth, the period has seen the development of a much more structured ecclesiology than that of our British counterparts. American Methodism became a *denomination* much sooner in its development than British Methodism. This movement from sect to church has resulted in a more formalized doctrine of the church together with a greater concern for *The Discipline.* This puts polity in a greater light than in Britain, and the priority can be noted even to the present. Our post-Wesley influences by choice and necessity have caused us to focus large amounts of time and energy on structural and institutional matters.

In bringing our theological heritage up to the present,

some important questions remain to be answered. First, what shall be the authority of pre-Wesley and Wesley influences? Second, is there some "organizing principle" in contemporary United Methodism that will allow us to take advantage of the past two hundred years of theology as Wesley was able to do with the centuries before him? Third, how shall we proceed in order to produce theological definition that avoids the pitfalls of legalism on the one hand and indifferentism on the other? Fourth, what is the relation between the schools and the church now that the majority of clergy are trained in seminaries to serve the denomination? Fifth, what should we do with pluralism as it has come to be expressed in the church today? Sixth, to what extent is it possible and/or desirable for United Methodism to become an alternative theology and community in society? Seventh, what kind of accountability and leadership is necessary for bishops, other church leaders, and boards and agencies?

In raising these questions we are recognizing the richness of our theological heritage, the power that comes through the union of knowledge and vital piety, and the potential renewal of the church for even greater service to God and the kingdom. At the same time, we are acknowledging the need to define our heritage more clearly so that we can better tell the world who United Methodists are through a theology-and-polity that more accurately expresses our identity. Our theological heritage flows into the present to remind us that we have both reason for rejoicing *and* room for improvement.

NOTES

1. The term was generally used in Wesley's day to refer to the first 450 years of church history, roughly covering the period from the close of the New Testament era to the Creed of Chalcedon.

2. Thomas Jackson, ed., *The Works of John Wesley*, vol. 10 (Grand Rapids: Baker Book House, 1979), p. 79. Hereafter this edition will be referred to as *Works* (Jackson). This same quotation is also printed in Albert Outler, *John Wesley* (New York: Oxford University Press, 1964), p. 195.

3. Wesley's relation to and use of the mystics is complex. In this case, we are referring to mystics like Thomas à Kempis, who emphasized the imitation of Christ as the goal of the Christian life.

4. Kenneth Rowe, ed., *The Place of John Wesley in the Christian Tradition* (Metuchen, N.J.: Scarecrow Press, 1976).

5. Frank Baker's *John Wesley and the Church of England* (Nashville: Abingdon Press, 1970) is the best single source for studying Wesley's relation to Anglicanism.

6. Quarterly Review Reprint Series has made this text available along with a very good introduction to the document. James White, ed., *John Wesley's Sunday Service of the Methodists in North America* (Nashville: United Methodist Publishing House, 1984).

7. Outler, *John Wesley*, pp. 121–33. The Pine edition of Wesley's *Works* contained these homilies (9:31–53). Subsequent editions dropped them.

8. Albert Outler, ed., *The Works of Wesley*, vols. 1–4 (Nashville: Abingdon Press, 1984–1987). This thirty-five volume, definitive edition was begun by Oxford University Press and subsequently continued by Abingdon Press. To date, four volumes of sermons, two volumes of letters, a volume of appeals, and a volume of hymns have been published. Hereafter this edition will be referred to as *Works* (Bicentennial). Abingdon has also published a convenient, one-volume edition of Wesley's sermons entitled *John Wesley's Fifty-three Sermons* (Nashville: Abingdon Press, 1984).

9. Steve Harper's *Devotional Life in the Wesleyan Tradition* (Nashville: Upper Room, 1983) focuses on the means of grace.

10. Outler, *John Wesley*, pp. 134–81; *Works* (Jackson), 8:275–338. Paul Chilcote has written a helpful contemporary examination of these three considerations entitled *Wesley Speaks on Christian Vocation* (Nashville: Discipleship Resources, 1986).

11. Robert Monk's *John Wesley: His Puritan Heritage* (Nashville: Abingdon Press, 1966) is a solid, detailed examination of Wesley's relation to Puritanism.

12. Ibid., pp. 157–67.

13. Recent Wesley studies have reemphasized Wesley's essential orthodoxy, e.g., Outler, *John Wesley*, pp. 119–20, and Colin Williams, *John Wesley's Theology Today* (Nashville: Abingdon Press, 1960), pp. 16–17.

14. Gerald R. Cragg, *The Church and the Age of Reason* (New York: Penguin Books, 1960).

15. "Speculative latitudinarianism" was a term that implied an uncritical, excessive embracing of variant theological positions. Wesley believed it was an unacceptable approach that resulted in doctrinal indifferentism. His sermon "Catholic Spirit" clearly shows his opposition to it.

16. Richard Heitzenrater's *Elusive Mr. Wesley,* vol. 2 (Nashville: Abingdon Press, 1984), shows how Wesley responded to his critics.

17. Outler, *John Wesley,* pp. 28–31.

18. Rowe, *The Place of John Wesley,* pp. 29–32.

19. Robert Chiles, *Theological Transition in American Methodism* (New York: Abingdon Press, 1965).

20. Thomas Langford, *Practical Divinity: Theology in the Wesleyan Tradition* (Nashville: Abingdon Press, 1983).

21. Douglas Meeks, ed., *The Future of Methodist Theological Traditions* (Nashville: Abingdon Press, 1985), pp. 34–52.

22. J. Bruce Behney and Paul H. Eller, *The History of the Evangelical United Brethren Church* (Nashville: Abingdon Press, 1979).

23. George Croft Cell, *The Rediscovery of John Wesley* (New York: H. Holt & Co., 1935).

24. Langford's *Practical Divinity* contains another helpful analysis of similar post-Wesley trends in our heritage, pp. 259–72.

Chapter 2

How United Methodists Think Theologically

Wesleyans in general and United Methodists in particular have not been considered theological heavyweights compared with traditions such as Lutheranism or Calvinism. There are some notable theologians in the tradition, but by and large the shapers of Protestant theology have not been Methodists.[1] To understand why, it is necessary to go back to Wesley himself. Even after two hundred years, Wesley's status as a theologian is still debated. He has never lived down the fact that he did not produce a systematic theology as some theologians did. His identification as a folk theologian has not endeared him to the academy. And the frustrating inability to put contemporary labels on him has made him both friend and foe, depending on where one stands. Consequently his heirs in theological circles have been at something of a disadvantage.

It is important to recognize that Methodists consciously do theology differently from some other denominations. That difference can be described as the attempt in Methodism to join knowledge and vital piety. It is a method that seeks truth using a broad range of persons and perspectives. We have tried to avoid the extremes of detached ivory-towerism on the one hand and shallow sentimentalism on the other. We have attempted to blend the insights of rational inquiry and personal/corporate experience. Here is one of the clearest demonstrations of our efforts to achieve unity of theology and polity. It is our historic affirmation that faith and life are inseparable. It is evidence that substance and structure must always be linked if both are to operate as they should.

This is admittedly a difficult task. It is walking a tightrope with the possibility of falling off either on the side of cold dogmatism or on the side of hot enthusiasm. This is all the more reason to consider *how* Methodists think theologically. And as we do so, we will see that it is a blending of creativity and constraint, independence and control. This topic will be approached by looking at our theological method in the aspects of spirit, standards, systems, and structure.

THE SPIRIT OF METHODIST THEOLOGY

A commitment to join knowledge and vital piety produces a certain "spirit" in our theology. It sets a tone that can be described in several ways. First, it fosters *eclectic openness.* From Wesley to the present, we have drawn widely from both Protestant and Catholic faiths. We can find points of agreement with every major theological tradition. This has led to Methodism's sometimes being caricatured as "blowing with every wind of doctrine." But it is more accurately a spirit of varied inquiry than of naïve indifferentism.

In this respect we are like John Wesley, who stressed that Methodists wanted nothing more than for the movement to be part of authentic Christianity.[2] Even today we like to bear witness to our ecumenicity whenever possible.[3] At times our eclecticism has created internal problems of identity and consistency.[4] We continue to struggle to identify a core of beliefs, and even when we come close, there is lively debate as to their authority. Nevertheless, we maintain that eclecticism is a laudable feature of our theological method even if it sometimes gets out of control.

This leads to a second feature of our spirit: *evangelical focus*. By this we do not mean evangelical as variously defined by conservative Christians in the past fifty years. Rather, we mean a spirit that focuses on fidelity to the early creeds and confessions of Christianity. More will be said about this later in the chapter. For now it is sufficient to stress a commitment to orthodoxy as an integral feature of our theological method.

However, it would be a mistake to interpret this evangelical focus in an antiquarian or obscurantist sense. It is not an attempt to champion any return to a previous period (e.g., a "back to the eighteenth century" movement). The objective is to champion a spirit of "renewal" using the principles of historic Christianity. The continual struggle is to find the proper blend of creativity and confessionalism.

Third, our theology has an *experiential dynamic*. It has a developmental nature. United Methodists seek to articulate theology in a way that follows the human journey. Traditionally we have found that process in the *ordo salutis*—the order of salvation. The order of salvation is a way of paralleling the story of grace with the story of growth. God's actions parallel the human journey. This approach helps to "locate" people theologically and chronologically. And when we have thus located ourselves, we have a means of knowing how to respond to God's grace for the rest of our lives.

This approach to theology has a dynamism that traditional, topical dogmatics often lack. It holds the gospel story in its proper flow, emphasizing the grace of God as it manifests itself in human experience. This careful blending of divine and human dimensions may well be one of Methodism's most significant theological contributions. The order of salvation provides an answer to the question, "Where and how do I fit into God's plan for the world?"

Interestingly, the answer to this question gives insight into the unity of theology and polity. The order of salvation connects theological substance and institutional structures. Our polity (at its best) is a tangible expression of how we respond to grace. Polity is a means of making concrete our conviction that there is "grace for all, grace in all." Polity enables us to manifest and apply particular aspects of theology to real situations. It is our medium for expressing theology in the world.

Fourth, our theology has an *evangelistic result*. Our goal is not information, but transformation. The purpose of theology is to persuade. We are on a mission to change persons and society. Wesley abhorred "dead orthodoxy."[5] He knew the importance of correct content, but he also knew that to stop with content was to destroy the very theology thus formulated. One of his favorite phrases was, "I offered Christ." His approach was soteriological—the salvation available through Christ. The evangelistic result gave early Methodism its substance and steam.[6]

This result is more comprehensive than the contemporary definition of "getting saved." It is more closely in line with the biblical definition of salvation, which is "wholeness." It includes the grand sweep of God's grace from creation to glorification. It includes and affirms the more narrow idea of new birth, but also points to significant aspects of God's work before and after conversion. Early Methodism is an example of a movement that kept a broad definition of salvation ever in mind. To say that our theology seeks an evangelistic result is to say that God wills wholeness for every person, that we stand against everything which destroys wholeness, and that such wholeness is possible only by the grace of God.

To speak of our theological spirit is a way of saying that our theology is considered. We think theologically in a way that reverences God and honors people, that celebrates holiness and humanness. We seek to do theology in a way that touches people and transforms them, enabling them to live abundantly and eternally. We want a theology that is responsive to the physical, intellectual, emotional, mental, and spiritual dimensions of life. It is this spirit that has led some to speak of our concern for "practical divinity."[7] We believe theology is intended to facilitate the formation of the life of God in the human soul. Our polity should help us achieve that basic intention.

THE STANDARDS OF METHODIST THEOLOGY

Like the wind, theology can blow in all directions. It can blow out of control; it can blow to no effect. A sound theological method requires some sense of definition, some agreed-upon standards, to guide it. Such standards provide specificity and direction. They are like a sail that catches the wind of the theological spirit and moves the church in positive directions. As United Methodists, we have such standards in place.

We begin with four early creeds as an expression of community with other Christians. Historically we have fully affirmed the Apostles' and Nicean creeds in our formal worship. Wesley added to them the Athanasian Creed and the Creed of Chalcedon. He highlighted the creeds of the early church because he felt they faithfully captured the essence of scriptural Christianity. Wesley spent precious little time defending or even expounding these creeds. He simply affirmed them as the superstructure that held Methodists accountable to and in connection with the broader Christian community.[8]

Two hundred years later, we continue to formulate theology in light of a continued affirmation of these historic creeds, plus some more contemporary statements.[9] We believe that the creeds provide a necessary point of reference in our theological task. It is true that individual theologians have at times departed from fidelity to these creeds, but the point is that this is done as a *recognized departure* from a longstanding, denominational commitment to the creeds of Christendom—commitment that United Methodists reaffirm each week in public worship.[10]

Second, certain theological confessions are used as further standards. It is clear that Wesley did not hold the confessions in the same light as the creeds. He felt at liberty to amend the Anglican Articles from thirty-nine to twenty-four by omitting some and editing others. In this respect, the Methodist Articles of Religion can be considered Wesley's clearest expression of theology in a confessional format.[11] Early American Methodists recognized this and adopted the Articles with the addition of the twenty-fifth article pledging allegiance to governmental leaders. It was the considered opinion of early Methodists that "these are the doctrines taught among the people called Methodists. Nor is there any doctrine whatever, generally received among that people, contrary to the articles now before you."[12]

The union of the Methodist Church and the Evangelical United Brethren Church in 1968 resulted in two official statements of faith: the Methodist Articles of Religion, and the E.U.B. Confession of Faith. The Uniting Conference declared both to be concurrent, authoritative statements of belief for the new denomination.[13] At the same time, the new body recognized that it was not strictly proper for one church to have two confessions. From 1968 to the present, the church has been exploring various ways and means of developing a new, single theological document for United Methodism.

Like Wesley, we feel a certain liberty to amend the confessions, but not in a way that results in a contradictory theology.[14] The Restrictive Rules place constitutional limits on the nature and extent of the amendment process or the synthesizing of the two previous documents into a new doctrinal statement for the church. Any new, single document must keep faith with previous normative confessions. If it does not, it will be a violation of the constitution of United Methodism. The proposed draft of a doctrinal statement for the 1988 *Discipline* clearly shows this by stating that "the heart of our task is to discern how seriously we take our distinctive doctrinal heritage and how creatively we appropriate the fullness of that tradition in the life and mission of the church today."[15]

Third, Wesley's *Standard Sermons* and *Explanatory Notes Upon the New Testament* are used as standards in our theological method.[16] The proposed doctrinal statement recognized this material as normative while noting that their juridical status has never been clearly established.[17] Wesley's *Standard Sermons* contain the substance of Methodist doctrine and stand much like the Anglican *Homilies* as examples of communicating theology in a homiletical medium.[18] The *Explanatory Notes Upon the New Testament* reveal Wesley's concern that Methodists know the Word of God.[19] Taken together, the sermons and the *Notes* reflect Wesley's purpose to communicate "plain words for plain people" and to do it in such a way that knowledge and vital piety are conjoined. These materials remain among our standards as living reminders of the substance of our major doctrines.

To speak of doctrinal standards is to remind ourselves that our theology is controlled. If these standards are affirmed, upheld, and faithfully used, they adequately serve as checks and balances on any tendency to produce theology in a free-lance, independent fashion. Furthermore, these standards provide a means of discerning the fidelity of contemporary theology. The fact that they continue to be afforded normative status reminds us that it is possible to distinguish between theology done in the Wesleyan spirit and theology which is not. As the church moves into its third century, these standards need new affirmation and attention.

THE SYSTEM OF METHODIST THEOLOGY

It would be hard to find a better name for our denomination than Method*ism.* John Wesley had a methodical personality, and as far back as the Oxford days, "Methodism" was a term used by eighteenth-century observers to describe the logical, systematic nature of the Holy Club. That same spirit and commitment has found its way into the present life and form of the church. Theologically speaking, we officially recognized that methodical bent by making the quadrilateral our disciplinary system for doing theology.

As an Anglican, Wesley already knew and used the trilateral: *Scripture, tradition,* and *reason.* His own faith journey and that of others, coupled with the influences of Puritanism and the Moravians, made the addition of *experience* natural, even necessary. Wesley was not ignorant of the consequences of making this addition, and he had to spend a significant amount of time and energy defending himself against charges of "enthusiasm"—a term of derision, roughly synonymous with our term "fanaticism." But he maintained that this addition and the use of a quadrilateral was the system for the Methodist movement. It remains so today.

Scripture

We begin with Scripture, for that is where all Christians begin.[20] In 1729, John Wesley was struggling to find the center of authority in his life. He came to the conclusion that there could be no other center except Scripture. He wrote, "I began not only to read, but to study the Bible, as the one, the only standard of truth, and the only model of pure religion."[21] Thirty-seven years later, he reaffirmed this commitment by writing, "My ground is the Bible. . . . I follow it in all things great and small."[22] On a number of other occasions, he made equally clear affirmations.[23]

In taking this position, he set Scripture above tradition, reason, and experience in terms of ultimate authority.[24] He fully recognized that these three had to be employed in the interpretation of Scripture, but never as substitutes or coequal facets in establishing doctrine. In this way he was a true reformer, holding to "sola Scriptura"—not in the sense of Scripture *only,* but rather Scripture *ultimately.*[25] This means that the quadrilateral is not equilateral. On a given issue or topic, it may be necessary or helpful to begin with tradition, reason, or experience, but the Bible is the final authority.[26]

Obviously this perspective does not answer all the questions about the Bible that are being asked today. Nor does it guarantee agreement on matters of interpretation. But it does reveal the commitment in Methodism to a high view of Scripture. This view is not bibliolatry, and it does not require a narrow definition of inerrancy to support it. Rather, it is the belief that God is a God of revelation and that such revelation has been communicated to humanity through the pages of Scripture. The Bible is the church's book for every age.

Tradition

Because it is the church's book, the church is charged with the holy task of interpreting the Bible's message to every generation. Thus tradition stands second in our theological system. Wesley refused to make tradition coequal with Scripture, but he used tradition as much as any theologian, and more than some. He preferred the tradition of primitive Christianity (A.D. 100–450), but reading lists reveal his indebtedness to later periods as well. He concluded that tradition is "highly serviceable in its kind and in its degree."[27]

The use of tradition places Methodism in the mainstream of Christendom. It is an expression of our commitment to "catholic spirit." Through it we gain perspective, confirmation, guidance, and discernment. It also fosters humility as we realize that we stand on the shoulders of giants who have walked with God and written about the experience. Tradition enables us to break out of a time-bound, culture-captured view of theology. It reveals where the church has stood in a wide variety of places over a long period of time. Tradition serves us well in determining whether our contemporary theology is faithful to the historic message of the gospel.

Reason

Reason comes third in the system. It is our way of saying that when we think theologically, we *think*. Both his personality and his ordination into the Anglican Church directed Wesley toward "reasonable faith." He believed that even after the Fall, reason was sufficiently useful to guide a person toward God. As a tool for interpreting Scripture, he wrote, "Now, of what excellent use is reason, if we would either understand ourselves, or explain to others, those living oracles."[28] He could no more omit the use of reason than any other human faculty. His considered position is seen in these words: "It is a fundamental principle with us that to renounce reason is to renounce religion, that religion and reason go hand in hand, and that all irrational religion is false religion."[29]

All this sounds like a man thoroughly conditioned by the post-Enlightenment perspectives that were dominant in eighteenth-century Anglicanism. But there were differences and limits for Wesley. He wrote, "Reason cannot produce faith, in the scriptural sense of the word."[30] Reason could never substitute for living faith. Christianity is rational, but it is not rationalism. Here is where other elements of the quadrilateral kept Wesley balanced in his theology. He never allowed reason to dominate his religious quest, much less to stand above revelation as some in his day did.[31]

Today reason serves us in calling forth discipline and care in formulating theology. Reason clarifies, organizes, and relates theology to the rest of human knowledge. Reason saves us from tunnel vision or producing theology in a vacuum. It enables us to enrich our theology with truth from other disciplines. The proper use of reason enables us to communicate the gospel in ways that are attractive and applicable to contemporary life.

Experience

Finally, our system makes use of experience. Having firmly established an objective dimension to his theological method, Wesley felt at liberty to bring experience into the picture. In fact, he felt it was a necessary addition if Christianity was to achieve its purpose of effecting life. He wrote, "What Christianity (considered as a doctrine) promised is accomplished in my soul."[32] Experience thus confirmed the realities of God's grace attested in Scripture. Experience is to the individual what tradition is to the church. It is truth made personal.

In a highly privatized, individualized age it is necessary to stress that experience is not synonymous with subjectivism or libertarianism. Experience is always informed by and accountable to the other dimensions of the quadrilateral. Methodist theology is not interested in producing private, ecstatic experiences. We do not hold to experience as a means of accelerating the "I–me" spirit of contemporary living. Rather, experience is that aspect of our theological method that enlivens, energizes, and animates our doctrine. It is the means to receive, appropriate, express, and describe our theology. It is our best guard against a dead orthodoxy.

To speak of a system in our theology is a way of saying that we seek to be comprehensive in our theological development. We believe the quadrilateral helps to achieve this goal. It communicates the interplay between God and persons. It balances objective and subjective elements. It is enriched by insight from the church and from the world. It engages the full range of human skills and senses. It draws on the past, but lives in the present. It is a system which holds that the essence of truth has been revealed in Scripture, but that the communication of truth is an ongoing task.

THE STRUCTURES OF METHODIST THEOLOGY

Theology is not created *ex nihilo*. It is not created by just anyone. It develops in and through the church by persons committed to the Christian faith. It develops in established structures as responsible parties engage in theological reflection and formulation. In United Methodism, a variety of groups are involved in critical and constructive activities related to our theological task. Critically, they test and evaluate various expressions of faith, asking if those expressions are true, appropriate, clear, cogent, and credible. Constructively, they seek to represent Christian faith authentically and convincingly to the present age.[34]

The Conference System

Basic to this process is the system of conferences. The General Conference is the only group officially allowed by *The Discipline* to establish doctrine for the denomination. "No person, no paper, no organization, has the authority to speak officially for The United Methodist Church."[35] That is the legal truth of the matter, but in practice other groups reflect our theology explicitly or implicitly. This is inevitable in a large, diverse denomination. It is inevitable when the General Conference only meets once every four years. But it is important to remember that General Conference *alone* can speak officially for United Methodism.

This is why the theological task of General Conference is so crucial. Theology inevitably shapes polity. Wesley recognized this as he structured early Methodist conferences to move from what to teach, to how to teach, to what to do. It is not to our credit when theological matters are given comparatively minimal attention. Instead, an authoritative theology should be communicated and implemented through appropriate programs. Between sessions of General Conference, all United Methodist people and organized groups within the denomination should be expected to act in ways consistent with the theological statement. The dual task of General Conference to establish and maintain doctrine is a task of highest priority.

But once the General Conference has acted, the theological task moves on to other bodies as well. Next in line come the jurisdictional and central conferences. These bodies are charged to interpret General Conference actions to their respective constituencies.[36] While these bodies do not officially or in theory establish doctrine, they practically and in fact do so through the programs they adopt and the emphases they place on them. It is easy to see how theology and polity interact at this level of the church. This is further emphasized by the election of bishops, who personify the theological spirit and substance of the denomination.

However, it is the annual conference that serves as the

basic body of United Methodism. It is from this body that delegates to general and jurisdictional conferences are elected. And it is at the annual conference that most general church policies and programs are received, interpreted, and implemented. Annual conferences have the power to expand general church decisions so long as additions do not conflict with or reduce official actions of the General Conference as spelled out in *The Discipline.*

Annual conferences become powerful interpreters of theology. History shows that interpretations can and do vary from conference to conference. As a strength, this demonstrates the willingness in United Methodism to let theology be applied close to home where opportunities and needs are most clearly seen. As a weakness, the process can produce a multiheaded "hydra effect" that results in a lack of denominational consensus on matters of faith and practice.

The conference system is the United Methodist attempt to make the theological task a representative enterprise without throwing it open to anyone and everyone. Through the conference system the church is in a perpetual process of adopting, evaluating, and revising major and minor points of theology. In this respect the theological task is never finished. Neither should it be up for grabs every time General Conference meets. A definitive and authoritative presentation of theology through established channels should have durability; and it should be respected by everyone in the denomination.

Boards and Agencies

While conferences are the primary bodies for establishing and appropriating the theology, they are not the entities that carry on the task most of the time. This function is actually carried out by representative boards and agencies and, from time to time, by task forces established to deal with a particular issue. Without doubt, the boards and agencies have gained power both in influencing the development of theological content and in determining how established doctrine is to be interpreted in the church. Boards and agencies operate at every conference level and in some cases include the districts. Thus they have pervasive influence.

Boards and agencies determine how to emphasize the quadrennial themes and policies enacted at General Conference. They determine what nuances to stress in each of the programs. They determine what resources to publish or to use in communicating those programs to the church. To the extent that they seek intentional consistency with established doctrine, they are carrying out their disciplinary responsibility. When they act independently in ways that alter or contradict established theology and polity, they step outside their intended function. In the past twenty years there has been increasing debate over the role of general boards and agencies, whether they are to be serving arms of the denomination or, instead, primarily prophetic and policy-initiating organizations.

The Caucuses

The power that the conferences and the boards and agencies exert has given rise to an unofficial structure for interpreting theology in the denomination: the caucuses.[38] These groups exist to advocate particular concerns. They usually highlight issues or groups that they feel the denomination is either ignoring or minimizing. They monitor the denomination when they perceive segments of it to be violating official policy in theology or polity. As such, caucuses play a prophetic role in the denomination. They serve a positive institutional function, although that function is often unappreciated. Caucuses keep the church on its toes. They keep pushing United Methodism toward what they perceive to be greater fidelity and efficiency. They keep the church from falling asleep.

By their very nature, caucuses run the risk of perpetuating a nonsubmissive spirit of never allowing the actions of General Conference to be fully binding. It is the nature of caucuses never to give up. This raises the larger issue of authority. Is it possible for United Methodists to establish official theology and polity that has denomination-wide status and authority? Are we at the mercy of every subdivision of the denomination (official or unofficial) to ignore, change, or contradict what the General Conference does? Is it possible to have consensus and durability? These are important questions that the existence of caucuses raises for us.

All this inevitably flows into the local church. Each congregation is the final link in our structural chain. Through the pastor, other staff, elected leaders, charge conference decisions, Sunday school curriculum, confirmation materials, and worship, the local church is where the theology is implemented through polity. The determinative action comes at the local church level. Nothing can substitute for vitality and fidelity here. The local church should be a place of ongoing, serious theological dialogue. It is the place where the gospel is proclaimed in word and deed.

Theology As Communal

To speak of structures is to say that our theology is communal. No person or group can establish doctrine independently. Through our conference system we decide what to teach, how to teach, and what to do. These decisions eventually trickle down to every congregation and church member for interpretation and implementation. To view our theological task in this way clearly reveals why it is such an awesome responsibility. The potential within Methodism is tremendous. When the church is at its best, theology becomes the medium for telling each other and the world the truth of God. And when United Methodists think theologically, that is what they are attempting to discover.

NOTES

1. Thomas Langford, *Practical Divinity: Theology in the Wesleyan Tradition* (Nashville: Abingdon Press, 1983). Interestingly, none of the persons mentioned by Dr. Langford is represented in the

recently published, fifteen-volume series *The Encyclopedia of Religion*, edited by M. Eliade (New York: Macmillan, 1987).

2. "Doctrinal Statements: A First Draft Proposal," *Circuit Rider* (February 1987): 10. The document begins with a section entitled "Our Common Heritage as Christians." This doctrinal statement, while not yet official, will be cited as the most up-to-date example of the attempt in United Methodism to prepare a statement of faith for *The Discipline*.

3. *Works* (Jackson), 8:346.

4. One of the places this most frequently occurs is in the ordination process, where candidates for ministry are interviewed and processed. While general denominational requirements are in place, specific requirements or interpretations of denominational policy vary from one annual conference to another. It also occasionally manifests itself as official boards and agencies differ among themselves as to "correct theology" for United Methodism.

5. *Works* (Bicentennial), 1:220.

6. Albert Outler, *John Wesley* (New York: Oxford University Press, 1964), pp. vii and 27.

7. "Doctrinal Statements: A First Draft Proposal," pp. 10–11. See also Outler, *John Wesley*, p. viii.

8. An interesting exception occurs in "A Letter to a Roman Catholic," *Works* (Jackson), 10:80–86. In this letter Wesley affirms the Apostles' Creed as a means of showing that Protestants are essentially one with the Roman Catholics in the main tenets of Christianity.

9. For example, the Korean Creed, the Modern Affirmation, and the Creed of the Church of Canada.

10. William H. Willimon, *With Glad and Generous Hearts* (Nashville: Upper Room, 1986), pp. 103–113.

11. Wesley also scattered brief descriptions of the basics of Christianity in his *Works*. See *Works* (Jackson), 8:46, 56, 67, 472; and 9:174. Curnock's edition of Wesley's *Journal* has summaries in 3:320, 534; and 4:419. The Telford edition of the *Letters* also contains some summaries in 4:146, 149, 159, 235–39.

12. "Doctrinal Statements: A First Draft Proposal," p. 12.

13. *The Book of Discipline of the United Methodist Church, 1968* (Nashville: United Methodist Publishing House, 1968), pp. 35–36.

14. Ibid. The first, second and fifth Restrictive Rules of our constitution are important to this issue. There has been lively debate about the meaning of the phrase "present existing and established standards of doctrine." Also, there has been a difference of opinion as to how much the Articles of Religion and Confession of Faith can be changed before something "contrary" is produced. Although the

issue is by no means settled, it reveals how seriously we take the confessions of the church. Paragraphs 16–20 of *The Book of Discipline, 1984* contains the Restrictive Rules. In our opinion, these rules are normative and must take precedence over any attempt to substantially "revise" the doctrinal statement. The Restrictive Rules were carefully placed in the constitution to ensure that any subsequent doctrinal statements are faithful to the content and spirit of the original Articles of Religion of the Methodist Church (1784).

15. "Doctrinal Statements: A First Draft Proposal," p. 12. Additional helpful insights into our relationship to doctrinal standards can be found in Thomas Langford, *Wesleyan Theology: A Sourcebook* (Durham: Labyrinth Press, 1984), pp. 273–90.

16. The *Standard Sermons* of John Wesley are available in the first two volumes of the bicentennial edition of the *Works*, published by Abingdon Press. In 1986, Zondervan reprinted Edward Sugden's older edition of the *Standard Sermons*. Wesley's *Explanatory Notes Upon the New Testament* was reprinted by Abingdon in 1983.

17. "Doctrinal Statements: A First Draft Proposal," p. 12. This issue has been debated by responsible Wesley scholars, with differing conclusions. Richard Heitzenrater holds that they are not legal standards in his article, "At Full Liberty: Doctrinal Standards in Early Methodism," *Quarterly Review* 5 no. 3 (1985). Thomas Oden maintains they are, in "What are 'Established Standards of Doctrine?' A Response to Richard Heitzenrater," *Quarterly Review* 7 no. 1 (1987). See also Oden's *Doctrinal Standards in the Wesleyan Tradition* (Grand Rapids: Zondervan, Francis Asbury Press, 1988).

18. *Works* (Bicentennial), 1:103.

19. Wesley expanded this commitment by publishing *Explanatory Notes Upon the Old Testament* in 1765. This three-volume edition never achieved normative status, and sales were comparatively low. However, they do further illustrate Wesley's desire for Methodists to be biblically literate and knowledgeable concerning the whole counsel of God.

20. "Doctrinal Statements: A First Draft Proposal," p. 13.

21. *Works* (Jackson), 2:367.

22. Ibid., 3:251. Bishop Mack Stokes has written a helpful book, *The Bible in the Wesleyan Heritage* (Nashville: Abingdon Press, 1979).

23. For example, in "The General Rules of the United Societies" (1743), in the Preface to the *Standard Sermons* (1746), in "A Roman Catechism, With A Reply Thereto" (not dated), and in Standard Sermons 11 and 27.

24. Mack Stokes, "Wesley on Scripture," in *Basic United Methodist Beliefs: An Evangelical View*, ed. James Heidinger (Wilmore, Ky.: Good News Books, 1986), p. 13.

25. Outler, *John Wesley,* p. 28.
26. Robert Tuttle, "The Wesleyan Quadrilateral—Not Equilateral," in *Basic United Methodist Beliefs: An Evangelical View,* pp. 19–25.
27. *Works* (Jackson), 10:75.
28. Ibid., 6:354.
29. *Letters* (Telford), 5:364.
30. *Works* (Jackson), 6:355.
31. William R. Cannon, *The Theology of John Wesley* (New York: Abingdon Press, 1946), p. 19.
32. *Works* (Jackson), 10:75, 79.
33. Ibid., 10:78.
34. "Doctrinal Statements: A First Draft Proposal," p. 13.
35. *The Book of Discipline of the United Methodist Church, 1984* (Nashville: United Methodist Publishing House, 1984), para. 610, pp. 275–76.
36. Ibid., para. 21–34, pp. 26–29.
37. Ibid., para. 801–2405, pp. 395–621.
38. Many caucuses are temporary in nature. Examples of more permanent ones include Black Methodists for Church Renewal, Good News, MARCHA (Hispanics), Affirmation (gays), NIAM (Asians), and the Methodist Federation for Social Action.

Chapter 3

United Methodist Doctrinal Emphases

Institutions live and move according to a sense of identity. In contemporary management literature, one of the principles of survival is to discover that identity and "stick to your knitting." Organizations use their identity to attract new constituencies and to expand existing markets. It is the way to increase and preserve their holdings.

With respect to the United Methodist Church, one key aspect of our "knitting" is our doctrine. While we seek to be one with other Christian denominations, it is inevitable that we will have certain emphases which give us a particular sense of identity. In this chapter we want to examine some of those doctrinal emphases.

At the outset we must remember that doctrinal emphases cannot be adequately described simply by excerpting distinctive terms, phrases, or ideas from a statement of faith. We have already seen that our theology is the overall product of the interaction between spirit and substance. So our examination of doctrinal emphases must necessarily consider both aspects.

THE UNITED METHODIST SPIRIT

We begin with matters of spirit. The atmosphere of our theology is as important as the content of it. Wesley recognized this early on in his determined effort to link holiness and happiness. And church history generally reveals that the attitudes of believers are highly influential in determining how the content of theology looks and sounds. In terms of communication and promotion, the spirit of our theology is extremely important. It becomes part of our unique emphasis.

First of all, we must remember that ours is a theology of mission. Methodism would never have become a vital movement had it remained confined to Oxford. There came a point when Wesley became convinced that God had raised up Methodism to revive the church and reform the nation. With that larger perspective and conviction, he went on to develop the content and structures of early Methodism that he felt would best achieve those ends.

The oft-quoted phrases of early Methodism demonstrate our emphasis on mission: "the world is my parish," "faith working by love," "spreading scriptural holiness across the land," "to spread true religion in these three kingdoms," and "I offered Christ." The journal and letters of Wesley reveal a man on a mission—a mission that attracted an increasing number of people. This missional motivation at least partly describes why Wesley chose preaching over lecturing, the order of salvation over traditional systematics, the open road over the academy. It also helps us to see why the United Societies, classes, bands, annual conferences, connectionalism, and ordination came to exemplify Methodism's polity. Each element was missional in some way.

When we look at our uniqueness, we must emphasize the continuing missional motivation. Our sense of mission continues to drive us. Institutional preservation, leadership development, church growth, theological education, quadrennial emphases, and all the rest are reflections of mission. If we sell our souls to anything other than what we believe God wills for Methodism to be and do, we will suffer. If we think more about careers than callings, we will have surrendered a precious part of our denominational emphasis.

Second, ours is a theology of love. Wesley's choice of Matthew 22:35–40 as the classic text of Methodism was not accidental. It was his way of consciously identifying with the holy living tradition of Christianity. He was setting the tone that would characterize the movement. It was a tone of "catholic spirit," which sought to rise above petty divisions over inconsequentials. It was a tone of community, where the only requirement for admission was "a desire to flee the wrath to come."[1] It was a tone of support and forgiveness, where members watched over one another in love. It was a tone of compassion, which always reached out to the "forgotten people" of society in ways that fed body, mind, and soul.

Methodists are sometimes criticized for going too far in this spirit of love. And it is true that we sometimes seem to prefer contemporary definitions of love to a more biblical meaning.[2] But even when we err, we have to admit that our motivation is to be as inclusive as the gospel will allow. We think in terms of "the many" and not "the few." The church is not a museum for saints, but a hospital for sinners. We are not trying to see how many we can keep out, but how many we can take in.

Admittedly this places great pressure on the church. On the one hand, we are pressured to reduce or blur our standards so that the church ends up looking little different from the world it exists to save. On the other hand, we face pressure to determine who we are, with as much clarity as responsible theology can produce. Constantly we face pressure to maintain a proper balance between such things as acceptance and accountability, continuity and change, sin and sanctification. But we accept this pressure as the inevitable pressure of love—pressure that cannot be avoided or codified. Our theology and polity both lose their heart if they are separated from our emphasis on love.

Third, ours is a theology of experience. This has been spoken of elsewhere, but it needs to be highlighted in the context of our emphases. Experience is the personal validation of our doctrine.[3] We are not ashamed to sing,

> You ask me how I know He lives?
> He lives within my heart.

At the same time, we are not those who accept any and all experiences as valid expressions of Christianity. We check our experiences against Scripture, tradition, and reason. And we submit our individual experiences to the wisdom of the community. But we do so celebrating the fact that the gospel of Jesus Christ can be known at the most personal levels of human existence. We are not content to stop with information. Formation is the goal—formation of men and women into the likeness of Christ.

Such experience leads inevitably to two further dynamics. First, it fosters an ecumenical spirit. We desire to link ourselves with all who experience Christ in their lives. Our participation in national and world ecumenical organizations and dialogues should not be surprising. We believe that any authentic experience of Christ will draw us closer to other Christians.[4] Second, our experience generates our evangelism. We know that God's search for us through Christ evolves into God's search for others through us. Our call to conversion becomes our challenge to evangelism. It is at this point when our experience comes full circle and becomes part of our missional emphasis. We stand in the great line of apostolic witnesses. Christian experience dictates that the church always be in an outreach mode.[5]

These elements of mission, love, and experience combine to produce the spirit in which we formulate the content of our theology and the structures of our polity. These elements of spirit form part of our overall doctrinal emphasis. In this atmosphere we develop particular expressions of faith. It is to these that we now turn.

A THEOLOGY OF GRACE

Much of our doctrinal emphasis can be summarized in the phrase "a theology of grace." We do not believe that grace is any particular property of Methodists, but we recognize that Wesley emphasized grace in ways that result in some distinctive doctrines. One of Wesley's most descriptive phrases in this regard is "grace for all, grace in all."[6] The first part of the phrase reveals Wesley's belief that no one is excluded from the operation of saving grace by some prior act of divine determination. The second part reveals the conviction that such grace is presently at work in every human being in some way. This operation of grace is described developmentally under four distinct headings.

Prevenient Grace

"Prevenient grace" is one of our most distinctive doctrines. It is the belief that God's grace is present in a person's life from the beginning and that this grace has a redemptive dimension. This is different from what Calvin called "common grace," which operates in every person, but not with any salvific dimensions. On the contrary, we believe that prevenient grace does everything common grace does, but also operates so as to move us to the place of repentance.[7]

It does this by "preventing" the absolute destruction of the *imago dei*. Even after the Fall and our subsequent participation in original sin, prevenient grace preserves in humanity authentic responsibility and sensibility. In other words, God's action through prevenient grace makes possible our re-action. As such, prevenient grace goes before any direct consciousness of God, any deep conviction of sin, or any discernible desire to please God. It is the "first light of dawn in the human soul."[8]

In terms of polity, the theology of prevenient grace can be seen in the entrance requirement for the United Societies: "a decision to flee from the wrath to come." This desire is akin to the first light of grace in the soul. The societies existed to provide a place for people who had made only this elemental step along the way. Their format provided basic exposition of Scripture, simple worship (especially singing), and a rudimentary system of accountability.

Justifying Grace

If prevenient grace is responded to positively, the next leg of the journey is "justifying grace." Here Wesley was closest to the Reformers. In this we gather together the doctrines of repentance, belief, pardon, new birth, regeneration, and initial sanctification. Taken as a whole, the experience of justification leads us through the experience of forgiveness and restores us to God's favor. But in all this there is a nuance that stands as one of our emphases; it is our belief that the righteousness which comes by faith is actual righteousness. It is not merely imputed righteousness; it is genuinely imparted righteousness. God not only declares us righteous, but we are made righteous with the righteousness of Christ. Wesley included the forensic notion of pardon, but went beyond it to speak of justification as actual transformation. He spoke of it as sanctification begun.[9]

The experience of justifying grace was most nearly provided for in the class-meeting structure. Records show that most people were converted in the class, not in coming forward in response to Wesley's preaching. Furthermore, there was usually a period of time between one's general awakening and actual conversion. The class meeting provided a smaller, more focused setting for bringing people to new birth and nurturing them in their basic post-conversion development. It also heightened the sense of accountability and became the primary missional body of Methodism. Lay leadership and personal sharing also enhanced one's response to justification.

Sanctifying Grace

Thus we move into the next stage of the journey: "sanctifying grace." With all Christians, Wesley recognized the gradual growth in grace that follows conversion and continues until death. In this sense he was guided by the general doctrine of holiness as ever-increasing maturation in Christlikeness. Within this gradual development Wesley included more specific doctrines of discipleship, nurture, and mission. Through the doctrine of sanctifying grace, our theology has as much to tell us about living after conversion as it does about getting converted in the first place.

Within this larger dimension of sanctification, Wesley included belief in "entire sanctification" or "perfect love," usually called a theology of Christian perfection. Here again, Wesley followed the guidance of holiness sources (especially those of Eastern Christianity such as the Cappadocian Fathers) that looked to a specific experience after conversion when a person established the intention to love God and others fully. On the basis of that depth commitment, such a person moved forward into life to reflect the interplay between intention and action. Wesley was so convinced of the importance of Christian perfection that he referred to it as the "grand depositum" of Methodism.[10]

Unfortunately, in the century after Wesley this doctrine became a source of contention and division. Much of it came over a misreading of what Wesley meant by "perfection." Even today people shy away from the doctrine because they mistakenly define Christian perfection as total flawlessness. This has sometimes been reinforced by loading the doctrine with various legalisms that appear to equate Christian perfection with certain acts of behavior. Interpreters out-Wesleyed Wesley, including in the doctrine aspects never seen in his own writings. The result was a separation of spirit and letter in the doctrine, so that Methodism's grand doctrine became our forgotten doctrine. The general result is that we have made the doctrine appear far less important than Wesley did.

Nevertheless, we are heirs of this doctrinal emphasis, and our order of salvation does not really make sense without a contemporary proclamation of holiness. When it is left out, we are without a theology of the nature and extent of human maturation in response to grace. Remove our doctrine of sanctification and we are cut loose from the major, classical sources of nurture in Wesleyan theology. And most of all, we are left without our historic means of describing the power by which we personally and corporately express our faith, ethics, and mission. Methodism stands in need of a fresh, contemporary, and forthright presentation of this doctrine.

The bands served as a structural facilitator of sanctification. Mutual confession, forgiveness, and encouragement characterized life in these groups. They were small enough to allow genuine personal directing toward greater maturity. They advanced holiness of heart and life and enabled people to "go on to perfection." In time, the structure of the bands was absorbed into the classes, but their purpose was never lost.

Glorifying Grace

Sanctifying grace carries us to the moment of death, where we experience God's grace in its glorifying dimension—"glorifying grace." Wesley came to say, "Methodists die well."[11] His own testimony at death confirmed the reality and preciousness of glorifying grace: "the best of all is, God is with us."[12] These words climaxed a long life where this had been the case, but more specifically they spoke of a deep reality in the hour of death itself. As such, they serve to summarize our belief in eternal life with the confident belief in the triumph of grace.[13]

Implications of the Theology of Grace

Because our theology of grace is so significant, a few concluding remarks must be made. First, we believe that this grace is resistible. At any point along the way people can and do thwart its purposes. This is why Wesley was no universalist.[14] However, a sober view of eternal destinies did not rob Wesley of a balanced and hopeful theology. He resolutely maintained that more people are won to faith by love than by fear. Therefore, because the gospel is good news, the most important word regarding all this is the word of salvation, not damnation.

The resistibility of grace has another important implication. It means that Methodists have never had to adopt a theology of predestination, which limits saving grace to the elect and which makes such grace irresistible. On the contrary, we maintain that every human being receives the gracious invitation to life and the gracious ability to move forward in that life. The *only* way not to enter heaven is by human default on that invitation. Here is another reason why close-knit structures for nurture and support were important in early Methodism. Wesley's theology and polity both develop out of a theology of grace. And at this point we have a case study in the integration of theology and ministry.

Second, we must not think of our theology of grace as containing different kinds of grace. Grace is grace. At every stage it is God's unmerited favor directed toward our redemption. This is the essence of grace. We name it variously to describe what it accomplishes, not to describe what it is. At different times grace does different things for us, but God does not give it in different amounts like money. God is not dispensing one type of grace at a particular time and withholding another type.

Grace is the atmosphere in which we live. It is living "in Christ" and allowing him to live in us. Grace is personal and perpetual. It is personal through Christ and perpetual through the Holy Spirit, who continually mediates grace to us. This means that grace is available all the time to meet our particular needs. All the potential of grace is present continually. No person can say, "I've received justifying grace, but God has not given me sanctifying grace." The only limitation of grace is our appropriation of it.

THE DOCTRINE OF ASSURANCE

As comprehensive as this picture of grace is, we have not captured every one of our emphases in it. Some other doctrines need mentioning. One of them is assurance. Wesley believed that a privilege of all believers is the witness of the Spirit with their spirits that they are the children of God.[15] The nature of such assurance must be clearly understood. It is the witness of a believer regarding *present* salvation, not a presumption about the future. Nevertheless, it is a glorious thing to be able to say in any moment, "I know that I am God's child!" And Methodists have maintained that this is a gift of God, available for any Christian.

At this point we must remind ourselves and others that this is not a test of the validity of our salvation. As Methodism expanded, Wesley encountered many who had authentic conversions, but who lacked assurance for a variety of reasons. He concluded that trials and doubts could prevent assurance from manifesting itself. So he refused to make the doctrine an essential. Yet he continued to proclaim it as an avenue to deep joy and confidence. It is an experience that contains within it the seeds of increasing intimacy and development.

THE IMPORTANCE OF DISCIPLINE

Along with assurance, we need to remember our emphasis on discipline. Growth in grace cannot occur automatically. Dietrich Bonhoeffer has reminded us that grace is not cheap. We do not experience its fullness without conscious and conscientious participation. Wesley described this divine-human synergism by saying, "God has worked, therefore you can work."[16] Hence, in Methodism we have a longstanding commitment to the disciplined life, and we have sought to provide structures where discipline can be cultivated. The instituted and prudential means of grace stand at the heart of our discipline.[17] They serve as another example of the unity of theology and polity.

Such discipline differs from works righteousness. We do not work in order to receive the favor and blessing of God. Rather, we work because we have experienced the grace of God. Furthermore, the coming of grace has enabled us to see that true faith is always applied and expressed. Use of the means of grace puts us in contact with the main channels by which grace comes, and it provides us with effective avenues to express our faith in life.

THE PEOPLE OF GOD

All this ultimately points to the church. While this is not a unique emphasis, it is an essential one. The church is the gathering of people for Word, sacrament, and order; it is the scattering of people for witness and service. It is the formative community in which we receive our identity, our enablement, and our mission.[18] This is why church growth and renewal must always be a priority. People cannot be developed right when the church is wrong. We cannot foster life if we are dead.

We believe that the life of the church is determined both by the vitality of particular congregations and by interaction among congregations. The latter manifests itself primarily through our connectional system, but also expresses itself in ecumenical relations. Through it all, we are witnessing to our mutuality and interdependency. The whole church is the body of Christ, and we are individually members of it.

Finally, we recognize that there will be special doctrinal emphases in every generation. The Holy Spirit moves certain things to center stage. What we have previously described relates primarily to the ongoing emphases of our denomination. Besides these, we see other aspects that need attention in our time—issues of peace and justice, for example. We must give ourselves to these issues with as much dedication as we give to ongoing emphases. Our challenge is to identify and address particular, contemporary accents in ways that do not ignore or erode our historic emphases. We must serve the *present* age, but not as if it were the only age.

Doctrinal emphases are inevitable in any denomination. They are our best efforts to describe particular aspects of the Christian faith. We would hope that our unique accents never become obstacles to fellowship and ministry with all who profess the name of Christ. We also hope that our emphases will both provide us with identity and provide the larger church with greater richness. It is in this spirit that we hold our emphases and offer them to others.

NOTES

1. *Works* (Jackson), 8:270.

2. Contemporary definitions of love frequently emphasize total acceptance with no recognition that someone may need to change. By contrast, a biblical definition of love includes total acceptance, but it does not omit the dimensions of accountability and improvement where needed.

3. Karl Rahner, *The Practice of Faith* (New York: Crossroad, 1986), pp. 21–23.

4. One of Methodism's chief exponents of ecumenism is Geoffrey Wainwright. His book *The Ecumenical Movement* (Grand Rapids: Wm. B. Eerdmans, 1983) is an example of his views. Colin Williams's *John Wesley's Theology Today* (Nashville: Abingdon Press, 1960) was written against the backdrop of ecumenism. Howard Snyder's *Divided Flame* (Grand Rapids: Zondervan, Francis Asbury Press, 1987) is a call to all Wesleyans to find renewed unity through an exploration of how their differences developed, especially in relation to the charismatic dimensions of our tradition.

5. George Hunter has sounded this note clearly in his books *The Contagious Congregation* (Nashville: Abingdon Press, 1979) and *To Spread the Power* (Nashville: Abingdon Press, 1987).

6. *Works* (Jackson), 7:373. Wesley's entire sermon "Free Grace" is especially helpful.

7. Ibid., 10:228–29.

8. Ibid., 6:509. See also Steve Harper's *John Wesley's Message for Today* (Grand Rapids: Zondervan, Francis Asbury Press, 1983), pp. 39–46, and the proposed Doctrinal Statements in the *Circuit Rider* (February 1987): 11.

9. Ibid., 7:205 and 8:284.

10. Wesley's doctrine of Christian perfection merits further, careful study. Albert Outler's *John Wesley* (New York: Oxford University Press, 1964) contains helpful primary secondary information: pp. 30, 33, 105, 108, 201, 217ff., and 251–305. Harper's *John Wesley's Message for Today* surveys the doctrine on pp. 91–104. Harald Lindstrom's older work, *Wesley and Sanctification* (London: Epworth Press, 1950), is a classic study on this topic.

11. In saying this, Wesley was also bearing witness to his own victory over fear of death that had plagued him in the earlier years of his life. The holy living tradition helped him through its emphasis

on holy dying, e.g., Jeremy Taylor, *Rules and Exercises of Holy Dying.*

12. Harper, *John Wesley's Message for Today*, pp. 107–114.

13. *Works* (Jackson), 5:171–84, 344–60, 405–412,; 6:189–98, 381–91; and 7:474–84.

14. Ibid., 6:382–83.

15. Ibid., 5:117–23. Wesley's correspondence from June through December 1738 contains numerous references to this doctrine. Robert Tuttle's *John Wesley: His Life and Theology* (Grand Rapids: Zondervan, 1979) also contains a helpful treatment of Wesley's doctrine of assurance.

16. *Works* (Bicentennial), 3:207–8.

17. David Watson's *Accountable Discipleship* (Nashville: Discipleship Resources, 1984) and Steve Harper's *Devotional Life in the Wesleyan Tradition* (Nashville: Upper Room, 1983) are two helpful sources for understanding discipline in the Wesleyan heritage.

18. William H. Willimon, *What's Right With the Church* (San Francisco: Harper & Row, 1985). He treats the same idea in two articles in *Christian Century*, "Making Christians in a Secular World" (22 October 1986) and "Answering Pilate: Truth and the Post-Liberal Church" (28 January 1987).

Chapter 4

The Church and the Sacraments

The church is both a producer and a product of theology. This is true at all levels of its institutional life. As we have seen, the General Conference is the only body in United Methodism that can officially establish theology, but its periodicity and temporary nature necessitate that every other part of the denomination become involved in the theological task.

The focus of this chapter is the local church. It is that part of Methodism which is most often encountered, and it is the most obvious place where theology and polity interact. The local church is the place "in which the pure Word of God is preached and the Sacraments duly administered according to Christ's ordinance."[1] The church will be examined from the standpoint of its ecclesiology and its role as a means of grace through the sacraments of baptism and the Lord's Supper.

WESLEY AND THE ANGLICAN BACKGROUND

The ecclesiology of Methodism grows out of its historic connection with Anglicanism, coupled with certain features akin to the free-church tradition. Both Anglicanism and free-church Protestantism were themselves products of the Reformation, which likewise emerged from Roman Catholicism. All this is to remind us that our ecclesiology is derived from a number of sources. Furthermore, our ecclesiology is missional in that it seeks to bring the message and medium of the church to bear on matters related to society and culture. Finally, our ecclesiology is a mixture of elements having roots in England and America. All this must be taken into account as we look at the nature and structure of the local church.

Our indebtedness to Anglicanism is sizable.[2] While a detailed examination of this is not possible in this book, the following characteristics of Anglicanism can be noted as having had special significance for Methodist ecclesiology: (1) Anglicanism retained the threefold order of ministry (deacons, elders, and bishops) begun in the primitive church, (2) it retained the liturgical and sacramental emphases of the church, (3) it perpetuated the Catholic understanding of the church as the mediator of God's grace, (4) it combined a spirit of conformity with one of latitude, and (5) it kept alive the idea of a state church.[3] In one way or another Methodism incorporated or reacted to these dynamics in the development of its ecclesiology. As such, it has a Catholic affinity, but not directly from Rome. And it has a Protestant nature, but not directly from the Continent.

John Wesley was nurtured in eighteenth-century Anglicanism by his parents and by an educational system that was integrally related to it. Anglicanism was the atmosphere in which he lived, so it is not surprising that he brought much of it into the early Methodist movement. But he was also an individualist who was not afraid to draw from a variety of sources to produce something he felt was better than any of its constituent parts. Thus Methodism came to represent an ecclesiology that was clearly a synthesis.

The uniqueness of Methodism was further enhanced by Wesley's perception of the movement as an agent of renewal within the Church of England, a perspective that necessitated its being something other than "status quo" Anglicanism. Standing within Anglicanism, it had to demonstrate an affinity with the parent church; but as a reforming movement it also had to offer clear alternatives to business as usual. This produced an ecclesiology that made enemies on both sides. Dissenters felt Wesley was too friendly to a decadent state church; institutionalists felt he had produced a renegade tumor in the body. His only option was to maintain that Methodism was little more than an expression of scriptural Christianity (something dissenters would like) and a manifestation of the true Church of England (something Anglicans would demand).[4]

Although he never fully satisfied extremists on either side, it is important to note that Wesley's commitment to the larger church was ultimately more determinative than a spirit of radical independence. He urged Methodists to attend services in the Church of England, and he himself did so. Whenever possible, he preached and administered the sacraments in Anglican churches. He fully subscribed to Article XIX of the Thirty-nine Articles, "Of the Church." He passed it on to the American Methodists as Article XIII with virtually the same wording.

It is in matters of interpretation that we begin to see some differences. Wesley's view of the church was more personal than that of his institutionalist contemporaries. For him the church was more a body than a building, in both theory and practice. Eighteenth-century Anglicanism had become enmeshed in its institutionalism. As Wesley quickly found out, the "best" ecclesiology of the day was unwavering loyalty to the church as it was. And while Wesley never minimized faithfulness to the established church, he did not make it the ultimate point in his ecclesiology. He was one with previous reformers in maintaining that the church is always capable of improvement, and he saw that as especially the case in his own church.

Wesley believed that the way to reform the church was by restoring the personal dimension. The church is a congregation of *faithful people* called together by God to embrace one Lord, one faith, one baptism, one God and Father of all.[5] Wesley interpreted this first in its most universal manifestations. His grand view of the church made the world his parish and saved Methodism from being ingrown and provincial in its ecclesiology. Working down from this worldwide view, he saw the need for many "parts" in the body of Christ, with Methodism being one of them. Within the larger church there would always be "little churches" to express true Christianity and to enrich the larger body.[6] Thus his ecclesiology was never developed so as to be a "one size fits all" understanding of the church.

Wesley felt at full liberty to bring together small groups of believers for mutual support, study, worship, accountability, and service. The United Societies format became his way of connecting and conserving the rapidly growing Methodism movement. Through this polity we see a clear expression of Wesley's theology and missiology. Methodism was his best attempt to replicate an ecclesiology confirmed by Scripture, tradition, reason, and experience. It was his way of expressing the personal nature of the body of Christ. At the same time, it was the structure for renewing Anglicanism and reforming the nation, the twin missiological tasks that he felt God had given to the Methodists.

At this point we see the free-church tradition influencing Methodism's development. Wesley's emphases on community and mission were both more nearly drawn from evangelical Protestantism in England than from the Church of England itself. To be sure, Wesley had seen both exemplified as a child in Epworth, but by the time of his graduation from Oxford these elements were largely carried by Christians outside the Anglican Church. The societies, while technically on the books of Anglicanism, were most often expressed in secular groups like the Society for the Reformation of Manners or in independent communities like those of the Moravians. By 1730, Wesley was convinced of the necessity of supportive community, and until his death in 1791 this feature was a hallmark of Methodism.[7]

This commitment to nurture and community was not the ultimate goal, however. Wesley knew that everyone does not experience community equally. Some people are outside of Christian community altogether and need to be included if at all possible. Furthermore, Methodist communities did not grow at the same rate or in the same way. Finally, needs within Methodism and in the larger society demanded that the movement have a social conscience. Very early, the principle of "a penny a week and shilling a quarter" became established, and this formed the first expression of our connectionalism.[8] So important was this sense of connection that some have viewed it as Wesley's greatest contribution to church polity.[9]

The remarkable thing is that Wesley never allowed the movement to become a substitute church. As Methodism grew, many came into the movement who had little or no knowledge of or appreciation for the Church of England. Many of these were the marginalized people whom Anglicanism had conveniently forgotten. But as long as possible, Wesley urged them, within the context of prudential means of grace, to attend all the ordinances of God offered by the church. For a long time he forbade Methodists to meet at hours that conflicted with Anglican services. Only as the Church of England increasingly distanced itself from the Methodists did Wesley take steps that ultimately led to Methodism's becoming a separate denomination in England after his death.

This commitment to remain within Anglicanism is especially noteworthy in our day, when independent movements have arisen and have soon become substitute churches, setting themselves up as superior to mainline denominations. Most of them have said or done things that early Methodism could have justifiably said or done. The difference is that Wesley's ecclesiology would not allow him to separate from what he felt was a legitimate part of the body of Christ, even if it was sick—*especially* if it was sick. He believed healing would come through those who stayed within, with the life of God in their souls. It seems clear that he would neither understand nor support separatism as it has sometimes been practiced in contemporary Christianity.

THE DEVELOPMENT OF THE CHURCH IN AMERICA

We must now begin to move from the English to the American scene. For what Wesley resolutely forbade in England, he allowed in America—i.e., the organization of a new denomination. The issue provides a point of transition as well as a means of exploring the ecclesiology that has developed in American Methodism in the past two hundred years. Specifically the issue revolved around Wesley's decision to ordain clergy for America, but in a much broader sense the decision reflects the first step toward the emergence of a new church.

Here we have one of the most interesting convergences of history, theology, and polity ever seen. Theologically Wesley was convinced that Holy Communion as a means of grace was an indispensable element in American Methodism. Years before, he had found a way to stretch the rubrics of administration with Anglicanism so that Methodists could still have the sacrament even though they were shut out of the church.[10] In doing so, Wesley was laying the groundwork for an even looser interpretation of church law regarding how clergy might become ordained to administer the sacrament. The point here is that the ordination issue was rooted in a theological conviction.

Historically the issue was made much more complicated than it might otherwise have been. Political tensions caused many Anglican clergy to return from America to their native land. Ecclesial tensions between the Church of England and Methodism made it impossible for Wesley to find a bishop who would ordain Methodist clergy for America. The revolutionary spirit in the colonies made it highly unlikely that Methodists who favored separation from England would be welcomed at Anglican altars in America. At the same time, more Methodists were migrating from England to the colonies. The result was that more and more of Wesley's "children" were cut off from the Lord's Supper, and the prospects of that changing were dim.

Only after much study and intense struggle did Wesley determine that a break from church law was acceptable under the circumstances.[11] An examination of the issue will reveal that Wesley did not act thoughtlessly, hastily, or without regard for possible consequences. It will also show that even people as near to him as his brother Charles opposed the decision. In the evolution of American Methodism, John's action has sometimes been viewed as something of a license for actions based much more in pragmatism than Wesley's really was. The end result, however, was that by 1784, American Methodists had a full-blown church, albeit in its institutional infancy.

The development came between the Declaration of Independence and the ratification of the Constitution. The only thing clear about the matter was that "freed" Americans would not accept political or ecclesiastical alliances with England except for Episcopalians who managed to survive the war and still hold a connection with the Church of England. On the whole, Methodists had been among those who saw separation from England as right and good, and who did not feel it wise or workable to continue official ties with British Methodism. Time and distance made a continued union organizationally impractical. The social climate made it intellectually unacceptable.

Wesley recognized the situation and allowed the separation to occur with his quiet blessing, mediated by Thomas Coke and Francis Asbury. The Christmas Conference of 1784 made a number of key decisions regarding the nature of the new church: (1) Methodism in America would be an episcopal church (much to Wesley's dismay), (2) it would have an itinerating ministry whose membership was in the annual conference, (3) it would establish local congregations, often as part of a circuit and always part of the connection, (4) it would take a structure sufficiently flexible to express the Methodist sense of mission in various places, (5) it adopted Wesley's vision of spreading personal and social holiness across the land, and thus (6) the Methodists understood themselves to be integrally involved in the development of the conscience and life of the new nation.[12]

These points are cited to show once again the close connection between theology and polity in the American church, just as we have seen the connection in British Methodism. There were, however, some differences in the two countries. For one thing, the American church was less liturgical. Wesley's edited version of the Anglican Order for Morning Prayers, offered to American Methodists as their "Sunday Service," never really caught on.[13] From the beginning, the American scene was more informal, and especially so as the frontier spirit was more and more expressed in a Methodism moving westward.

The American church was also less sacramental. In the beginning at least, this was probably due to the unavailability of the sacraments as compared with the frequent communion of British Methodists. American Methodists came to accept long periods without the sacrament as they continued to hold to a belief that only ordained clergy could properly administer the sacraments. And again, the frontier spirit put the emphasis on preaching more than the sacraments as the camp meeting became the main evangelistic arm of Methodism even before Asbury's death.

Thus American Methodism had both similarities to and differences from its English parent as far as polity was concerned. In theology, however, there was much closer agreement. Along with the proposed Sunday Service, Wesley had also sent over an edited version of the Anglican Articles of Religion, reduced from thirty-nine to twenty-four. These were readily adopted, with the addition of Article XXV, which affirmed Methodist allegiance to the new American government. These Articles of Religion served Methodism as its official, unalterable theological core until 1972, when they (along with the E.U.B. Confession of Faith) were given a new status as "landmark documents" and United Methodists began their long search for a new, single statement of faith.

What this means is that American Methodism carried on in its theology the same kind of catholic and evangelical emphases that had been part of British Methodism. Catholic emphases included a preference for prescribed order, an episcopal structure, concern for an ordained ministry, and continuity with the sense of authority residing in historic Christianity. Evangelical emphases included a commitment to nurture by the use of lay men and women, and a strong sense of community as over against a preference for rigid institutionalism.

These are important reminders for those who wrongly attempt to paint a picture of early American Methodism as having no real concern for theology or for a polity rooted in theological perspectives and convictions. The theological roots are clear and present from the beginning. The expressions of those roots reveal a polity designed to achieve theologically defined goals. All this was carried on with as much concern for the uniqueness of the American setting as Wesley had given to social forces in England.

UNITED METHODIST ECCLESIOLOGY

In the ensuing two hundred-plus years, Methodists have seen their ecclesiology altered by modifications, divisions, and unions. With the emergence of United Methodism in 1968, we entered a new phase. Is our ecclesiology still consistent with what has been described? For the following reasons, it is possible to answer in the affirmative.

First, we can note that a number of foundational documents include statements in keeping with our heritage. These include the Preamble to the Constitution of the church, Article XIII of the Articles of Religion of the Methodist Church, Article V of the Confession of Faith of the Evangelical United Brethren Church, paragraphs 201–4 of the 1984 *Discipline*, and the statement regarding the church that the pastor reads in the service of Confirmation and Reception into the United Methodist Church. Each of these documents reflects a connection with our historic ecclesiology.

Documentary statements, however, ultimately become real when they are expressed in the regular life of the church. Early American Methodists ordered their church in ways consistent with basic theological convictions. Furthermore, the uniting conferences in 1968 intended to remain consistent with our historic ecclesiology. The subsequent two decades have seen a marked increase in secularism, relativism, subjectivism, and pluralism in ways that church leaders could hardly have foreseen or planned for. And in varying degrees the church has been caught up in wildly fluctuating social forces, sometimes precariously near to the point of making new divisions.

The question at present is not, "Is United Methodism truly united?" The answer to that is a clear, mutually agreed no. The question for our time is, "Are we trying to be united, in ways that are consistent with the spirit and substance of our tradition?" It is possible to advance an answer of yes, although at present it is difficult to say with certainty that our attempt will be successful.

There are other significant signs that we are seeking an ecclesiology that blends theology and polity into workable expressions while at the same time consciously connecting with our heritage. First, we can note the way in which *The Discipline* itself is organized. Theological and missional tasks precede structural descriptions. For a long time we have been telling ourselves by the way we publish *The Discipline* that our ecclesiology is supposed to grow out of theological and missional concerns.

Second, our concepts of theology, mission, and ministry are undergoing thorough revisions by commissions mandated by the General Conference of 1984. Discussions with members of these commissions reveal the difficulty in coming to a consensus on these important issues. Early drafts have demonstrated how widely pluralism can and does express itself in our denomination. But as the task proceeds, it is moving United Methodism toward what will hopefully be clear, contemporary expressions of belief in these three important areas. We need the identity that such statements can provide as well as appropriate authority for such statements to guide the church into its third century.

Third, our bishops are beginning to speak out on theological, missional, and polity issues. It is important for the bishops to assume this teaching authority for the denomination, an authority that is consistent with the understanding of the episcopacy in the early church. Such actions move the bishops more into the role of moral and spiritual leaders in addition to their being institutional administrators.

Fourth, the past decade has witnessed a renewal of interest in and appreciation for the early Methodist tradition. Significant work in Wesley studies in particular and Wesleyan studies in general has revealed the value in reconnecting with our heritage. These efforts are not an attempt to go back to some supposed "good old days," but rather a recognition that our historic commitment to scriptural Christianity is always relevant and essential to a vital church.

We cannot expect that such things will result in lock-step conformity within United Methodism. Such constricted legalism would be a violation of our heritage, which has always sought to maintain the delicate balance between regulation and liberty. However, an increasing number of United Methodists are hoping that we will see a move away from open-ended pluralism and a return to a proper sense of authority, responsibility, and abiding values. Failing this, we can only expect to be blown about with every wind of theological and social change.

THE SACRAMENTS

At the heart of every ecclesiology is the worship of God. The primary purpose of this chapter is to examine the sacramental life of the church as it relates to ecclesiology. Such examination suggests a central facet of United Methodism and a key ingredient in our renewal: when we are at our best, we are a sacramental people.

Theologically this flows directly from our emphasis on the primacy of grace, as described earlier. Wesley's emphasis on the instituted and prudential means of grace as the usual means through which God communicates preventing, justifying, and sanctifying grace to people has also been discussed. The point here is not to repeat a discussion of the sacraments as means of grace, but to consider how baptism and the Lord's Supper inform and relate to the polity of the church.[14]

To do this we will use a contemporary paradigm showing the connection between story, belief, and action.[15] This paradigm states that story shapes belief, and belief shapes action. The sacraments of baptism and the Lord's Supper function at the level of story, serving as primary, regular means of telling the story of salvation in the midst of the congregation. This becomes very important for the Christian community, especially in helping us to remember the saving actions of God on our behalf.[16]

In infant baptism we tell the story of God's prevenient grace, which precedes the individual's knowledge of it or conscious response to it. We declare God's intention that none should perish and that through water and the Spirit our deliverance is being accomplished. We further bear witness to the essential role of the formative communities of family and church in the salvation process. And we look forward to the day when the infant will grow to the point where he or she can accept personally God's offer of salvation and be confirmed as a responsible member of the church.

In adult baptism we normally tell the story of conversion, since such baptism usually follows some kind of conversion experience. Added to everything we tell in the baptism of infants and children is the dimension of volition as the adult consciously chooses to accept the grace of God and to witness to it in the midst of the congregation.

In Holy Communion the emphasis is on the sanctifying, nurturing grace of God, which continually works in our lives to make us more conformable to the image of Christ. We also recognize that anyone who is at the place of repentance is a proper recipient of the Lord's Supper, and thus we bear witness to our belief in God's willingness to justify through the sacrament as well as sanctify.

Every time we tell the story by means of the sacraments we are repeating something old and experiencing something new. Each baptized person is a new demonstration of the saving grace of God. Every time we commune we experience God's grace at work in new places in our lives. Through the sacraments we are telling each other and the world that we are people of the New Covenant.

The story thus provides the framework for our identity. On the basis of our identity we develop our beliefs. And in our paradigm, belief includes our credos, policies, goals, and strategies. Finally, we use our beliefs to determine our actions, which both nurture the Christian community and evangelize the world.

Using this paradigm we can see how essential the sacraments are for the church. They are foundational and determinative. This is why an eroding of sacramental life in early Methodism or a minimizing of the sacraments today is most unfortunate. Failure to administer the sacraments properly over a long period of time must be included as a cause of our confusion and relativity in matters of faith and practice. The renewal of worship in general and sacramental life in particular is of utmost importance. For this reason, producing a new hymnal, complete with a revised liturgy and ritual, is a key event in determining the meaning of Methodism.

The life of the church at the local level is what ultimately gives United Methodism as a whole its vitality and identity. A proper ecclesiology is essential to our meaning and renewal. The issue is not so much high church or low church as it is *the* church. Its formality or informality is clearly secondary to its understanding of its nature and mission. Forms will and should be flexible enough to respond to particular situations. But running throughout United Methodism there needs to be a common thread of identity and purpose.

NOTES

1. *The Book of Discipline of the United Methodist Church, 1984* (Nashville: United Methodist Publishing House, 1984), "The Articles of Religion of the Methodist Church," article XIII, p. 58, and the "Evangelical United Brethren Confession of Faith," article V, p. 64.

2. For further study see Rupert Davies and Gordon Rupp, *A History of the Methodist Church in Great Britain*, vol. 1 (London: Epworth Press, 1965), and Frank Baker, *John Wesley and the Church of England* (Nashville: Abingdon Press, 1970).

3. Dennis Campbell, "The Relationship of United Methodist Theology of the Church to the Structure and Organization of the Local Congregation" (Unpublished article, pp. 3–5).

4. Albert Outler, *John Wesley* (New York: Oxford University Press, 1964), pp. 141–43, 312–14, and 384–424.

5. *Works* (Jackson), 6:392–401.

6. For more on how the principle of "*ecclesiola in ecclesia*" operated in early Methodism, see Egon W. Gerdes, *Informed Ministry* (Zurich: Publishing House of the United Methodist Church, 1976), pp. 76–78, and David Watson, *The Early Methodist Class Meeting* (Nashville: Discipleship Resources, 1985), pp. 80–91.

7. Watson, *The Early Methodist Class Meeting,* and also his book, *Accountable Discipleship* (Nashville: Discipleship Resources, 1984).

8. Howard Snyder, *The Radical Wesley* (Downers Grove, Ill.: InterVarsity Press, 1980), p. 55.

9. Davies and Rupp, *A History of the Methodist Church in Great Britain,* 1:230.

10. Anglican clergy were allowed to administer Holy Communion to the sick and a few of their friends. Wesley took advantage of this privilege to administer the sacrament to Methodists who were sick and a few of their friends, sometimes numbering in the hundreds!

11. The issue of Wesley's authority to ordain may well be the major problem he left his successors to debate. Several sources shed helpful light on the subject: Frank Baker, "Wesley's Ordination," *Proceedings of the Wesley Historical Society* 24, pp. 76ff.; Colin Williams, *John Wesley's Theology Today* (Nashville: Abingdon Press, 1960), p. 223ff.; and Edgar W. Thompson, *Wesley: Apostolic Man* (London: Epworth Press, 1957).

12. Campbell, "The Relationship of United Methodist Theology of the Church," pp. 16–19.

13. James White, ed., *John Wesley's Sunday Service of the Methodists in North America* (Nashville: United Methodist Publishing House, 1984).

14. Ole Borgen's *John Wesley on the Sacraments* (Nashville: Abingdon Press, 1973; Grand Rapids: Zondervan, Francis Asbury Press, 1986) is the best contemporary study of Wesley's views of baptism and the Lord's Supper.

15. Craig L. Emerick, "Repertoire and Rhythm: Leadership Styles and the Demands of Pastoral Ministry," *Perkins Journal* (January 1987): 28–43. Additional information about this paradigm can be found in John R. Sherwood and John Wagner's *Sources and Shapes of Power*, Into Our Third Century Series (Nashville: Abingdon Press, 1981).

16. Donald Saliers, *Worship and Spirituality* (Philadelphia: Westminster Press, 1984).

PART II

HOW UNITED METHODISTS ORDER THE CHURCH

Chapter 5

The Connection

The United Methodist people perceive their church as being a connectional system. This is a theological concept that is manifest in the way the denomination is structured and functions. It assumes that Methodists share a common understanding of the nature and mission of the church and the ways they as individuals relate to the various parts of the denomination. Connectionalism is one of the unique ways in which theology and polity are inseparable in Methodism.

COMPONENTS OF CONNECTIONALISM

There are three components to Methodism's understanding of connectionalism. The first is a sense of the entirety of the denomination. Every member has a feeling of being a part of the whole church. Therefore the individual holds membership in the entire United Methodist Church, not just in a local congregation. The total church is perceived to be greater than the sum of its parts.

The second component is an individual's sense of responsibility for the whole church. Although people join a specific congregation and give their primary loyalty to the local group, everyone is expected to support the work of the denomination. In practice this means contributing to various benevolent and mission projects administered by agencies and institutions related to an annual conference or to the general church. The reverse is also true; the regional and national organizations have a responsibility to both the local congregations and individual United Methodists.

A third component is the willingness on the part of individuals and congregations to be subject to the disciplined life and direction as determined by the denomination through the action of the appropriate leaders and official bodies. This centralized control goes back to the early days of Methodism when John Wesley was the authority for the movement. The class meeting was a group whose members were subject to the scrutiny and discipline of the leaders. The members were responsible both to their leaders and for the spiritual well-being of one another. Thus the societies and the individuals were in connection with each other.

Bishop William R. Cannon described the beginning of Methodism's connectional system as follows:

> The young church's connectionalism came directly from John Wesley. . . . His organization functioned from the center to the circumference. His helpers were deployed by him wherever need arose. . . . No society was independent. The direction agency for all of them was the conference. It decided policy and program and determined the means of implementing same.[1]

Methodism in the late twentieth century is very different from what it was in the days of John Wesley or Francis Asbury. The high level of discipline found in the early societies no longer exists. Nevertheless, a willingness to accept the direction of the church as expressed through the actions of leaders and fellow Christians remains a component of the connection.

The church is both an institution called of God and a voluntary organization. People have the freedom to accept or reject its demands. Adherents must be willing to accept the authority of the leaders and the official bodies. The denomination may determine the standards for membership and the structure that every local church must maintain. The people must accept the legitimacy of these actions and be willing to abide by them. In the final analysis, no one can be forced to do anything. The church has no sanction to impose on lay members other than expulsion, an option that is virtually never exercised.

The United Methodist connectional system is, therefore, a voluntary association of people and congregations who believe they have been called of God and have accepted certain standards for personal and group life. They believe it is an appropriate way for them to express their faith and grow in the Christian life. They are convinced it is an effective way for individuals, congregations, and the entire denomination to carry on the mission to which God has called them.

EXPRESSIONS OF CONNECTIONALISM

The United Methodist Church expresses its self-understanding as a connectional system in four ways.

General Superintendent or Bishop

The first expression of connectionalism is in the person of the general superintendent or bishop as an official of the entire denomination. *The Discipline* states that the "task of superintending The United Methodist Church resides in the office of bishop and extends to the district superintendent."[2]

In the early days of the denomination, the bishops were present at every session of the annual conferences. As the church grew and the number of annual conferences increased, not all the bishops could attend each one. So the bishops rotated among the annual conferences. The time when the annual conferences meets is still set by the bishops, and the published schedule of their meetings is called "the schedule of episcopal visitations." At first the bishop could reside wherever he desired; later on, he was assigned to an area; eventually the city of residence was designated.

The election of bishops by the jurisdictional conference and their subsequent service within that jurisdiction have regionalized the office to some extent. Nevertheless, they are still viewed as officials of the entire denomination, a reality symbolized by the practice of having a bishop from each jurisdiction participate in the consecration of every newly elected bishop.

District Superintendent

A second manifestation of the connectional system is the office and person of the district superintendent (previously called "the presiding elder"). This official serves as the visible connection between the local church and the denomination. The district superintendent serves as representative of the bishop in consulting with the congregation and the minister about pastoral appointments. He or she presides over the charge conference at which local church officials are elected, the budget adopted, and major program and policy decisions made. The district superintendent has the responsibility to mediate any disputes arising between the congregation and the pastor. He or she also has the task of informing the local churches of the denominational programs and benevolent causes and of urging their support. In a real sense the district superintendent is the most visible link between the local congregation and the rest of the connection.

Ministerial Membership

A third expression of connectionalism is the minister's membership in an annual conference rather than in a local church. The clergy members of the annual conference have the final determination as to who shall be admitted into the ministry. The typical minister will spend his or her career serving churches within an annual conference. The loyalty of the clergy tends toward the larger group, i.e., the annual conference or the entire connection, not the local church. Ministers still itinerate in the connection even though they may relocate only every four to eight years.

The Book of Discipline

A fourth manifestation of the connectional system is *The Book of Discipline of The United Methodist Church.* This book is probably the most significant factor in maintaining the connection. *The Discipline* is published every four years following General Conference. It contains the bylaws for all parts of the United Methodist Church.

The Discipline also contains some historical material such as a list of all the persons who have ever served as bishop, a brief historical statement, a doctrinal statement, and the social principles. However, the major portion of the book is given to defining the organization of the church. It sets forth the structure that each local congregation is required to have. It lists the local church officers and defines their responsibilities, and does the same for the annual, jurisdictional, and general conferences and the general boards and agencies. The qualifications for ministers and the process by which persons enter the ministry are spelled out. *The Discipline* defines the structure and function of every part of the denomination from the small rural church to a general board with worldwide responsibilities.

The content of *The Discipline* is determined by General Conference, which, subject to certain Restrictive Rules contained in the constitution, has virtually unlimited power.[3] Actually much of the content of *The Discipline* is carried over from quadrennium to quadrennium with no or only minor changes. Changes tend to be evolutionary as the bylaws are adjusted in the light of experience or to meet new situations. However, from time to time a General Conference will make major changes, as in 1972 when the organization of the general boards and agencies was drastically altered.

The Discipline ensures that all United Methodist congregations have the same form of organization. Local churches do not develop their own constitutions or bylaws. Ministers must meet the same criteria to qualify for membership in an annual conference. *The Discipline* requires that all parts of the connection be organized in the prescribed manner. It assures a degree of uniformity throughout the entire connection. Thus *The Discipline* is both an important factor in making Methodist people aware of their connectionalism and a practical tool in giving that system a high degree of uniformity.

REQUIREMENTS FOR CONNECTIONALISM'S CONTINUANCE

The continuation of the connectional system will depend to a great degree on three factors. The first is the maintaining of a degree of consensus among the United Methodist people concerning the nature and purpose of the church. This is required of any voluntary organization, whether religious or secular. The members are expected to contribute their time and talent; they must feel that the results are worth the effort. They must believe in the organization in which they invest themselves.

The Methodist connectional system has been built on a high level of consensus among its adherents. It assumes that the members share a general understanding of the nature and mission of the church and that they have joined together to further commonly agreed goals. For Methodism, which perceives itself as a denomination in which all persons are a part of the whole, such consensus is essential. This is quite different from a congregational type of church where the authority is clearly in the local group. In some denominations the congregation and the pastor can determine the extent to which they will or will not participate in the support and program of the denomination. Such an option is not possible for United Methodist congregations and ministers. If United Methodists are to accept the centralized authority as lodged in the General Conference there must be some degree of agreement concerning what the church is about, what it believes, and what it should and should not do.

This is not to imply that a connectional system requires a high degree of uniformity. Methodism has had a tradition of "think and let think." The denomination has been proud of its freedom of inquiry and its willingness to try new things. Nevertheless, there must be at least a broad underlying consensus on the fundamental nature and purpose of the church.

If an organization changes direction radically, it may not retain the loyalty of persons who are not in sympathy with the new direction. This will result in a lowering of the level of consensus and can cause severe strain. In its extreme form it can result in schism if segments of the constituency reach the conclusion that a consensus is impossible. When this occurs, the establishment of separate organizations may be perceived as the only alternative.

The second factor necessary for the continuation of the connectional system is a high level of trust among the various parts of the denomination. Methodism has traditionally delegated a great deal of authority to its several conferences and to certain officials. The church members must trust those in official positions, and the leaders must likewise trust their constituents. The laity trust the clergy to admit only those into the ministry who are called and who demonstrate that they possess the gifts and graces for the task. The congregations and the ministers trust the bishop to appoint clergy to places where they can most effectively serve the church. The Methodist people trust the general boards and agencies to carry on programs and support activities that are consistent with the United Methodist understanding of the Christian faith. Because all participation is voluntary, people and organizations can be in connection only when a high level of trust exists among all concerned.

A third factor essential to maintaining connectionalism is

a sense of mutual responsibility. United Methodist people and organizations must accept responsibility for all others in the system. One segment cannot live unto itself. Accepting responsibility for the entire church demands a willingness to contribute one's time, talent, and resources to help the church fulfill its calling. This willingness to serve is based on a general consensus concerning what the church is about and on the mutual trust of persons throughout the denomination. The acceptance of this responsibility and the specific actions that flow from it are the ways Methodist people implement their faith.

The Methodist connectional system has been effective because the laity and clergy have been willing to give priority to the church's witness and ministry over their personal needs and desires. Laypersons have given their time and talent; they have faithfully supported their church and its programs. Ministers have served where they were sent; all are expected to be faithful to the gospel and the Wesleyan heritage and to be responsible to each other. As long as this continues, the United Methodist connectional system will remain vital and effective.

NOTES

1. William R. Cannon, "Permanent Deaconate an Anomaly," *United Methodist Reporter* (27 April 1984): 2.
2. *The Book of Discipline of The United Methodist Church 1984* (Nashville: United Methodist Publishing House, 1984), para. 501.
3. Ibid., para. 16–20.

Chapter 6

The Ministry

The church is commissioned to minister in the name of Jesus Christ. The United Methodist Church shares in that commission and expresses it through its theology and polity. We encourage and equip men and women for ministry in a variety of ways and for a variety of purposes.

Ministry is rooted in the nature and activity of God as revealed in the Old and New Testaments. Scripture shows God to be ministering through communication of His Word, acts of deliverance, establishment of covenants, and the meeting of human need. The ultimate expression is the Incarnation, when Christ came among us as one who serves. During his lifetime, he gathered a body of believers whom he increasingly formed into a ministering community. On the Day of Pentecost, that body received their empowerment for ministry through the Holy Spirit. The rest of the New

Testament describes how they developed and expanded their ministry into the world.[1] Church history further expands, interprets, and explicates a theology of ministry.

THE GENERAL MINISTRY

Drawing from this theology, United Methodists affirm with Christians everywhere the priesthood of all believers. We believe every Christian is a minister of Jesus Christ within the context of his or her vocation. This is known as "the general ministry of the church" and is the foundation for all true ministry.

Our Wesleyan heritage reveals the indispensable role of lay ministers. This was true of early Methodism in both England and America, especially through the class leaders, exhorters, and lay preachers.[2] The clericalization of Methodism was a subsequent and secondary development. To the extent that it dominates the contemporary church, it is a move away from our primary theology and original polity.

Additionally, recent renewal movements (e.g., the lay witness mission, the evangelical revival, and the charismatic movement) have largely been generated and sustained by the laity. Christianity's millions remain its driving force. The laity represent the church's mission and message in places clergy never go and in ways clergy can never duplicate. Thus we must begin our examination of ministry by emphasizing the ministry of the laity.

We recall that one of the primary tasks of clergy is to equip the laity for the work of ministry in their spheres of influence (Eph. 4:11). Through worship, education, and support we consecrate and direct this massive ministry. One key to our renewal is a new emphasis on the ministry of laity.

Such ministry could be enhanced through periodic dedication services in the local church, where the laity would be affirmed and sent forth to minister in Jesus' name. This would expand the traditional dedication services that recognize lay officials within the church. Services of worship could easily include regular testimonies by laity as to the nature and results of their ministry. Congregations could regularly and specifically pray for the ministry of the laity going on every day in the week. In many churches people in similar vocations could be grouped together for sharing and support. Things like this would enable us to bear more faithful witness to our belief in general ministry.

THE REPRESENTATIVE MINISTRY

At the same time, we recognize that God calls certain persons to full-time ministry in the church and that such ministry frequently includes ordination. This is known as "the representative ministry." Here again, Methodists believe they are consistent with Scripture and the Wesleyan tradition. The Bible recognizes apostles, prophets, evangelists, pastors, and teachers as permanent offices in the church. And it recognizes that men and women will function as deacons and elders in their various ministries.

John Wesley made use of ordained persons whenever possible, especially in the administration of the sacraments, the preaching of the gospel, and the general oversight of the United Societies.[3] It is wrong to think of Methodism in any sense as an anticlerical movement or later as a church that minimized the need for clergy. Our task is to view ordained ministry in its proper relation to the general ministry and in ways that generate vitality and effectiveness.

To do this we must begin with the call of God. A sense of calling is essential for the clergy. It provides perspective, reminding one that supernatural tasks require supernatural power. A sense of calling serves as a source of strength when one is faced with questions about ministry. A sense of calling is a witness to the rest of the church that God assigns people to specific tasks. It is a challenge that should motivate every Christian to ask, "God, to what are you calling me?" Thus Methodists believe that the church suffers whenever an affirmation of calling is minimized or made light of.[4]

In a clericalized church it is important to set this call in context. The call to ordained ministry is not a "special calling" that creates a hierarchy of Christians. Rather, it is a *specific* call that defines our place—the place of service. Furthermore, it is not a unique calling. Every believer should live with a sense of God's direction. And a call to ordained ministry is not automatically permanent. This is clearly seen as many clergy move from one type of ministry to another across the years of their lives. It will also be true of some who are called to ordained ministry for a shorter period of time, either as a second career or as a first career that eventually leads to a nonordained vocation.

The essential matter is to face all circumstances with a careful sense of calling, properly interpreted and supported. In the United Methodist Church this means implementing a rather long process of helping people discover, develop, and respond to their callings. Actually the process begins at baptism, as the church bears witness that the child belongs to God and will be used to accomplish God's will in the world. In a mysterious sense every baptism is an ordination to general ministry.

In more practical terms, the church raises the possibility of ministry at the time of confirmation. Young people are helped to realize that they are ministers of Jesus Christ and that some of them will express their ministry through full-time service in the church. It is very important to raise these possibilities with people who are beginning to consider vocational options.

Persons in the general ministry are supported by the church through its historic commitment to higher education. By providing numerous colleges and universities, the United Methodist Church recognizes the variety of ministries and the need to prepare men and women for their vocations from a Christian perspective. This is perhaps the greatest demonstration of our theology of general ministry, and we must insist that our schools do their work with a clear sense of connection to Christianity and the church.

People who choose representative ministry are guided by the candidacy program. In late high school or college, men and women who wish to explore ministry as a vocational option are encouraged to go through this program. The candidacy program facilitates further study of the church and ministry as well as observation, interviews, and (in some cases) limited participation.

Through this process people discover several basic options. First, they discover the possibility of serving as a local lay pastor. This nonordained category of service may be full- or part-time and is restricted to service in a specific congregation.[5] Second, they see the possibility of serving as a diaconal minister. Again, this category is nonordained, and it is focused on ministries of love, justice, and service. It may be practiced within a local congregation or in a church-related agency.[6] This diaconal ministry was established in 1976 and replaced the consecrated lay workers who were employed full-time in a variety of church-related occupations. The third basic option is ordained ministry. In this category persons have all the service dimensions of diaconal ministry, with additional responsibilities of Word, Sacrament, and Order.[7]

It is not possible to describe in detail all the particular manifestations of these basic categories.[8] Suffice it to say that they contain many more expressions than the traditional descriptions of clergy as pastors or missionaries. If we are to express the possibility of representative ministry to people properly, we must be careful to expose them to the wide variety of options. And we must guard against implying that one kind of ministry is better than another.

Since it is true that the vast majority of persons choose some type of ordained ministry, additional attention will be focused on this process. In the United Methodist Church, ordination and acquisition of ministerial membership operate on parallel tracks. Institutionally speaking, acquisition of membership in an annual conference is the overall process, with ordination as a liturgical act performed at certain points along the way.

A person who completes the candidacy program has made the first step toward membership. Such a person moves from being an "inquiring candidate" to being a "declared candidate."[9] This means he or she has an official relationship with a charge conference and a district committee on ordained ministry. The district committee is responsible to help the candidate through suitable educational programs, usually including degrees from a college and a seminary.

Depending on specific goals, candidates become probationary members as the next step in their journey. For those in seminary, probationary membership begins when one-half of their work has been completed. This stage of membership is usually accompanied by the first ordination as deacon.[10] As a deacon, the minister is now authorized to conduct divine worship, preach the Word, perform weddings and funerals, and administer the sacraments if serving as pastor of a local church.[11]

Probationary membership continues through the completion of one's education and into the first or second year of actual service in an annual conference. This final phase of the membership process is supervised by the conference's probationary committee of the board of ordained ministry, with other appropriate persons involved at the local and district levels. Upon satisfactory completion of the probationary period, the person is admitted into full membership and usually ordained an elder. As an elder, the minister is given the expanded tasks of Word, Sacrament, and Order—applicable anywhere in the world, under proper appointment. Henceforth the member in full connection maintains accountability through the charge conference and in relation to his or her district superintendent.

ORDINATION AND APPOINTMENT

With this general view of conference membership, a look at ordination and appointment follows. In its essence, ordination is the church's acknowledgment that persons are indeed fit for ministry. It is the liturgical act that places people in the apostolic succession. As United Methodists we have two ordinations, each conferring specific duties and privileges.

Moreover, the church is stating through ordinations that ministers are responsible for rightly handling the gospel, properly administering the sacraments, and competently administering the overall work of the church. As ordained persons, clergy are responsible for passing on the faith to those who succeed them. Thus ordination is a conferral of responsibility by the church and an acceptance of responsibility by the ordinand.

In terms of ordination, it is important to remember that there are only two orders of ordained ministry: deacons and elders. Neither district superintendents nor bishops nor any other church leaders are ordained to their specific tasks.[12] In this sense we affirm that ordained ministers share a common community and a common mission. As such, clergy become responsible to exhort one another to growth in grace and to support one another in the stresses and demands of ministry. There are varied functions but a common fellowship.

As our denomination has evolved, our concept of ministry has become so increasingly complex that the 1984 General Conference established a commission to study the issue and eventually make legislative recommendations.[13] Among its many tasks, the commission must deal with obvious yet difficult questions:

> Where do local lay pastors and diaconal ministers fit into the scheme?
>
> What about associate members and appointees beyond the local church?
>
> What about guaranteed appointments?
>
> What is the proper relationship between ordination and the process of acquiring conference membership?
>
> How can we reconcile an overlap in function among local lay pastors, deacons, and elders that blurs their distinctions?
>
> Is our concept of ministry in harmony with Scripture, the Wesleyan tradition, and other denominations?

These questions call for careful consideration if we are to have the best possible representative ministry. But alongside such study there is also a need to look at the part-time, local lay pastor. This category holds untapped potential for United Methodism. Such persons could enhance our total ministry in a number of ways. They could serve churches too small for a full-time minister, but not located so as to be included on a circuit. They could serve in developing congregations that need to exist but cannot yet afford full-time ministers. They could serve in churches that need additional staff but cannot afford to employ full-time persons. They could relieve ordained ministers while they take much-needed sabbaticals. In short, lay pastors could become the very persons who could help the church accomplish many of its stated goals.

A renewal of part-time lay ministry requires careful study and implementation. In some cases it could be resisted by clergy who see it as a threat. Nevertheless, it deserves attention as we move into our third century. Such ministries would bring us back into greater harmony with biblical and Wesleyan concepts of ministry and would provide certain institutional advantages.

Standing above the whole picture is the matter of appointability. Ours is a "sent" ministry rather than a "called" ministry. United Methodist ministers are appointed by bishops; they are not invited by congregations. In recent times, as our society has moved to a greater emphasis on autonomy, independence, equality, and individualism, this system has been viewed by some as outdated and irrelevant. Clergy strain under it as appointments influence a spouse's ability to work, a family's ability to own their home, and so on. Laity react to varying interpretations of the consultation process by which the bishop and/or district superintendent must confer with the pastor and pastor-parish relations committee when an appointment is made.

We have declared ourselves to be a church that appoints its ministers, and the system is still workable. This does not mean it is beyond modification or improvement. Our appointive system has always sought to be appropriate for the times, but clergy have always been sent to a pastoral charge. Persons entering full-time ministry need to be fully apprised of the strengths and weaknesses of the system and be prepared to live in it. Congregations must not be allowed to have ultimate authority to make appointments or to handpick their next pastor. The appointment system will work most of the time when all parties act with proper assertiveness, intelligence, and compassion.

Given that, it is time to move toward longer appointments. In a highly mobile, often rootless society, clergy can make a significant witness to family life and stability by staying longer in a place. Moreover, in a depersonalized society that increasingly expresses distrust of religion, it takes longer to establish trust and credibility. A commitment to a longer appointment would help bond a pastor and a congregation. It would reduce the likelihood that either party could adopt the attitude "no need to make a deep commitment, since the relationship will not last long."

There are problems in longer appointments from an institutional point of view. It would disrupt the seniority system that presently operates. It would shift the center of the relationship away from the conference and bind pastors more closely to congregations. It would not so easily reward mediocrity. "Problem clergy" would have to be addressed in ways other than moving them frequently. In the long run, longer appointments would improve the quality of ministry.

The church exists to minister. The quality of our ministry is directly related to the vitality of our ministers. Here is where our best theology must inform and direct the development of our best polity. The church cannot tolerate deterioration in concepts of ministry without grave, long-term consequences for the denomination. To be in ministry (general or representative) is a holy privilege and an impossible task. Only the grace of God can produce the kind of ministry we need. And the best news of all is that grace is exactly what God offers for the making of ministers.

NOTES

1. "The Nature and Ministry of the Church," *Circuit Rider* (May 1986): 8–9; and "The Ordering of Ministry," *Circuit Rider* (January 1987): 4.

2. Wesley's *General Rules of the United Societies* (1743), *Rules of the Band Societies* (1783), and *Directions Given to the Band Societies* (1744), in *Works* (Jackson) 8:269–74, show the multiple

ministries of laypeople. See also William H. Willimon and Robert L. Wilson, *Rekindling the Flame* (Nashville: Abingdon Press, 1987), pp. 98–99.

3. Gerald O. McCulloh, ed., *The Ministry in the Methodist Heritage* (Nashville: Board of Education of the Methodist Church, 1960), pp. 11–31.

4. Richard A. Hunt and Joan A. Hunt, *Called to Minister* (Nashville: Abingdon Press, 1982), pp. 32–34.

5. *The Book of Discipline of The United Methodist Church, 1984* (Nashville: United Methodist Publishing House, 1984), para. 406–411.

6. Ibid., para. 301–318.

7. Ibid., para. 439.

8. Descriptive material is found throughout *The Discipline,* and a variety of publications is available from the Board of Higher Education and Ministry, P.O. Box 871, Nashville, TN 37202.

9. *The Book of Discipline, 1984,* para. 404–5.

10. Ibid., para. 413–417.

11. Ibid., para. 433.

12. Ibid., para. 501–533.

13. The work of the commission to study ministry is going forward, but specific legislation for *The Discipline* is not anticipated until 1992.

Chapter 7

Churchwide Decisions

Most decisions in the United Methodist Church are made by groups of people. These bodies are called conferences. They exist at several levels of the denomination from the charge conference in each local church or circuit to the General Conference with responsibility for the worldwide organization of United Methodism. Individuals are sent as delegates to these conferences and are authorized to act on behalf of the denomination.

The system of conferences has its roots early in the history of American Methodism. Although the first societies were organized by laypersons who had been associated with similar groups before coming to the colonies, they soon requested Mr. Wesley to send preachers. He responded positively. These persons organized Methodist societies throughout the colonies. John Wesley, of course, directed the movement in America, but distance made it impossible to exercise the degree of control that was possible in Britain.

With the end of the Revolutionary War and the coming of independence for the United States, the separation of American Methodism from the British organization was inevitable. The Methodist Episcopal Church was formally organized at the Christmas Conference of 1784 in Baltimore. The participants were the clergy who assumed the authority to found the church. The decision was made collectively by those able to attend, which included most of the ministers. They acted on behalf of all the Methodist people in America. Conferences continue to make decisions in their areas of assigned responsibility on behalf of the now-called United Methodist people.

The growth of Methodism soon brought about changes in the organization. The growing membership and the size of the country made it impossible for all the clergy to meet every year. So the church was divided into regions, and the ministers serving a region met every year. Thus the annual conferences came into being. However, all the ministers for a time continued to be eligible to attend the nationwide meeting that was held every four years. Within a quarter of a century (1808) it was necessary to have a delegated general conference, because the membership and the country were too large for all the ministers to attend the quadrennial meeting. Persons were selected by the various annual (geographical) conferences according to a formula that would ensure proportional representation. This system of delegated conferences has continued to the present. It has been modified by the addition of laypersons and by changes in the rules of what a particular conference can and cannot do, but fundamentally conferences continue to be the basic decision-making bodies in Methodism.

It is important to note that the denomination organized in 1784 was called the Methodist Episcopal Church. The church was to have general superintendents or bishops. Although Francis Asbury had been appointed a superintendent by John Wesley, he wisely allowed himself to be elected by the preachers, thus assuring that his authority was thoroughly based in the action of the conference. The creation of an episcopacy with life tenure also assured a degree of continuous tension between the bishops and the General Conference and, in the last third of the twentieth century, between the bishops and the general boards and agencies. Much of Methodist history from the O'Kelly Schism in 1792 to the division of the church into northern and southern branches in 1844 to the debate over term episcopacy in 1976 has revolved around the power of the bishops.

Nevertheless, the concept of the conference as a body to make decisions is basic to Methodism. It rests on the theological assumption that Christian people working together can, under the guidance of the Holy Spirit, make the best decisions for the church. It assumes that those persons selected as delegates to the various conferences will to the best of their ability make the choices that will enhance the Christian witness and ministry.

Obviously not all decisions are made by a conference. The appointment of a pastor to a charge is the responsibility of the individual bishop. The constitutionality of a General Conference action is reviewed and determined by the Judicial Council. However, most policy decisions are still made by the delegates assembled in conference. When Methodism acts or speaks, it is done by a group of persons delegated and authorized to do so. This chapter will examine how decisions for the broad areas of the church are made, including the worldwide (but largely American) General Conference, the five regional jurisdictional conferences in which the church in the United States is organized, the central conferences, the regional structure of United Methodism elsewhere in the world, and the Judicial Council.

THE GENERAL CONFERENCE

The most important gathering of United Methodism is the General Conference. This group of one thousand delegates, one half of whom are clergy and the other half laity, meets for eleven days in April or May once every four years.

It is customary to rotate the place of meeting among the five regional jurisdictions.

The practice of having the highest legislative body meet quadrennially has resulted in United Methodists operating on a four-year cycle. Much energy and effort is expended in preparing for and attempting to influence the General Conference, particularly in the twelve to eighteen months preceding the meeting. Any major changes must be approved by the body, whether it be a modification of the organization of the congregation, changes in requirements for ordination, or allocation of the national church budget.

General Conference is a gathering of the United Methodist family. Although it is largely an American institution, enough delegates from outside the United States are present to make it clear that the denomination is worldwide. The gathering can be described as a combination of a revival meeting, class reunion, political convention, and county fair. Elements of all are present.

A large number of people will attend in addition to the one thousand delegates and the reserve delegates. These will include the bishops, the Judicial Council, members of general agencies, administrators of the theological schools, representatives of the various caucus groups who are present to lobby for their particular causes, and members of the secular and church press. Spouses of many of the participants will be present. Some clergy and laypersons will attend at least a part of the conference simply to witness the event.

Various meetings will be scheduled at the site of a General Conference. National church organizations of various kinds will meet because many participants are to be present. The theological schools will have meetings of their alumni.

A General Conference is both businesslike and festive, and always strenuous. While the delegates will spend long hours in legislative committees and plenary sessions, there will also be worship services with opportunities to hear some of the denomination's leading preachers. There will be music and dramatic presentations.

Powers

The Constitution states, "The General Conference shall have *legislative power over all matters distinctively connectional. . . .*"[1] This authority is spelled out to include the definition and conditions of church membership; the requirements for and the powers of the clergy; the powers and duties of the annual conferences; the powers, duties, and privileges of the episcopacy; and the authority to revise the hymnal and rituals, to provide a judicial system, to initiate and direct all connectional enterprises, which include all of the general boards and agencies. The General Conference also has the authority to determine and provide for raising and distributing the funds required for the work of the denomination.

The various actions of the General Conference are incorporated into *The Book of Discipline*. This volume, containing the bylaws under which all parts of the church operate, is published every four years immediately following the General Conference.

The General Conference is the only body that is authorized to speak for the church. *The Discipline* states that "No person, no paper, no organization, has the authority to speak officially for The United Methodist Church, this right having been reserved exclusively to the General Conference under the constitution."[2] The various positions and statements coming from the body are published in *The Book of Resolutions*.[3] This volume gives the denomination's official stand on scores of religious, social, economic, and political issues. The material in *The Book of Resolutions* is not church law, but rather the positions that the General Conference hopes the Methodist people will support.

Membership

The Constitution provides that the membership of the General Conference may range from six hundred to one thousand persons, with the body itself setting the figure. The total has been set at the maximum for several quadrennia.

The General Conference has been a delegated body since 1808. The delegates are elected by the annual conferences with the number being proportional to the strength of the conference. The current formula calls for one clergy for every fourteen ministerial members of the annual conference and an additional delegate for each major fraction thereof. There is also one clergy delegate for each 44,000 church members and major fraction thereof. The total number of lay delegates is equal to the number of clergy delegates.

Delegates are elected at the sessions of the annual conferences preceding the General Conference. Ministerial delegates are elected by the clergy, and lay delegates by the laity. There are no nominations; members vote for any eligible person. The first several ballots are an informal nominating process as persons see who is receiving support.

Electing General Conference delegates is a matter of great interest and much campaigning, both subtle and not so subtle. Caucus groups (such as women, blacks, or rural pastors) try to ensure that someone from their group is elected. An aspirant to the episcopacy must be elected early, if not first, to be considered a credible candidate.

The campaigns for a place on the General Conference delegation can be intense, particularly among the clergy within the annual conference. The election process is a way of demonstrating who are the leaders in the annual conferences. To be selected by one's peers to represent the annual conference is an indication of the person's stature in the body.

The Petition

Any United Methodist organization, minister, or lay member may send a petition to the General Conference. Literally thousands of petitions dealing with a wide range of subjects are received by that body. Some petitions are serious, are carefully prepared, and deal with significant issues. Others border on the frivolous.

The General Conference must deal with all the petitions. Each is assigned to a legislative committee, which tends to vote "nonconcurrence," either because it does not approve of the petition or because the subject is to be dealt with in some pending legislation. Petitions that come from a general board or agency are likely to get serious consideration. Those from individuals, local churches, and other organizations tend to receive only the most perfunctory treatment. Given the tens of thousands of petitions, there simply is not time to deal with each of them.

Instead of being a viable method by which to introduce specific legislation or propose a United Methodist stand on a social issue, the petitions provide a kind of informal referendum on what the church members are thinking. If several hundred petitions on a given subject are received from individuals and churches across the country, it indicates that a significant segment of the constituents desire some specific action by the General Conference.

Several proposals have been made to screen the petitions so that only a manageable number will be forwarded to the General Conference. These have included requiring petitions to be first approved by a local church charge conference or some other official body. The General Conference to date has refused to impose any restrictions, so that any United Methodist individual or organization may submit any number of petitions directly to the General Conference.

Functions

In the space of less than two weeks the General Conference enacts the legislation under which the United Methodist Church will operate for the ensuing four years. It takes official positions on a wide range of issues in the larger society. And it does this with no staff assistance other than a secretary, whose major task is to publish the minutes.

The delegates spend most of the first week meeting in several legislative committees that will prepare material to be considered by the entire body. The General Conference will approve the vast majority of recommendations approved by the legislative committees. A few, however, will be subject to intense debate. Occasionally a legislative committee will present majority and minority reports, and the entire body must decide between them. As the time for adjournment approaches, much action is taken with little or no debate as the conference rushes to finish on schedule.

Veteran observers refer to the "mood" of a particular General Conference. Early in the session it becomes possible to predict the kinds of legislation the body will and will not approve. Because there is simply not time to consider the implications of the multitude of proposals, a General Conference will tend to ratify the consensus that the church has already reached. If the specific issue is controversial, it will have been discussed in various contexts and debated in the church press. At some point a General Conference will settle the issue and the denomination can move on to other matters. In 1976 the General Conference debate over a limited term for bishops was decided in favor of life tenure. The long debate over ordination of homosexuals was decided when the 1984 General Conference passed a clearly stated prohibition.

The importance of an action by a General Conference is clearly understood by those who want to influence the church. This explains why so much lobbying is done by the caucus and special-interest groups. It is questionable how effective these are at the national level, because a General Conference will reflect the consensus to which the denomination has already come.

THE JURISDICTIONAL CONFERENCE

The United Methodist Church in the United States is divided into five regions known as jurisdictions. They are a relatively late addition to the denominational structure, having been added at unification in 1939. No part of the denomination was the cause of more controversy during the quarter-century after 1939 than the jurisdictional system.

Two of the major issues faced by the three branches of Methodism as they moved toward unification in the twentieth century had great significance. The first was how to enable the Methodist Episcopal Church South to avoid feeling that it would be overwhelmed by the larger northern church. The second was how the black congregations, located largely in the former Confederate states but part of the northern church, would relate to the unified denomination. The jurisdictional system was the compromise arrangement that probably enabled the three branches of Methodism to merge. The southern branch of Methodism was able to maintain a degree of autonomy; the regional jurisdictions were given the power to elect the bishops who were to serve in the region. The black annual conferences were placed in a sixth jurisdiction that overlapped the five others. This Central Jurisdiction ensured the election of black bishops and members of the boards and agencies. It was also perceived, until its dissolution in 1968, as Methodism's version of "separate but equal."

Regional Differences

In northern and western Methodism, the jurisdictional system was seen by many as a compromise with the forces of racial segregation. In the South it was defended as necessary to maintain denominational unity and as a way to develop programs on a regional basis. Thus the Southeastern and South Central jurisdictions have staff and own assembly grounds that are the site of many regional activities. While there are jurisdictional organizations and programs in other parts of the country, these have been much less extensive than in the South. Furthermore, the merger of the black and white annual conferences between 1968 and 1972 has removed the stigma of a segregated jurisdiction, thus allowing for the development of regional activities without the feeling that segregation is being perpetuated.

The jurisdictional system is no longer needed to provide for the black annual conferences. However, there is ample evidence that a regional organization serves a valuable purpose. The United Methodist Church is so varied that the denomination needs a structure which can make allowances for regional differences. Although it is occasionally suggested that they be abolished, the likelihood is that the jurisdictions will continue indefinitely.

Membership

The number of members of a jurisdictional conference is computed by having one ministerial delegate for every seven ministerial members of an annual conference or fraction thereof and one for each 22,000 church members or fraction thereof. The number of lay delegates will equal that of the clergy. In practice this means that the persons elected as delegates to the General Conference plus an equal number will comprise an annual conference's representatives to the jurisdictional conference.

The size of the jurisdictional conferences will vary according to Methodist strength in the region. The Southeastern Jurisdiction is the largest; the Western, the smallest.

The five jurisdictional conferences are required to meet simultaneously, which has been in mid-July following the General Conference. The place of the meeting may vary although it will be within the particular jurisdiction.

Functions

The function of the jurisdiction that captures everyone's attention is the election and assigning of the bishops. This event represents the culmination of months of speculation, anxiety, and no small amount of campaigning. It is without doubt the high point of the meeting.

The jurisdictional conferences also elect the members of the boards of managers of the national boards and agencies. These are the persons responsible for the denominational bureaucracy. Given the role which these organizations play in setting priorities, determining how national church funds shall be spent, and controlling the church's channels of communication, the election of board members is an extremely important task.

A jurisdictional conference determines the boundaries of

the annual conferences. The only stipulation is that an annual conference must have a minimum of fifty ministerial members in full connection. The merger or realignment of annual conferences must be approved by the conference. This can be the subject of controversy, as evidenced by recent proposals in various sections of the Northeastern Jurisdiction.

THE CENTRAL CONFERENCES

In territory outside the United States, the annual conferences and other mission conferences may be organized into central conferences. There are seven of these around the world that are an integral part of United Methodism.

The central conferences function much like a jurisdiction. They consist of several annual conferences and provisional annual conferences. They elect bishops who are members of the Council of Bishops. They may establish boards to carry out programs appropriate to regions where they serve. They determine the boundaries of the annual conferences within their areas. Because the central conferences operate in a wide range of social and cultural settings, they are authorized to make rules and regulations for the administration of the work within their areas as conditions may require. This includes changes and adaptations of *The Discipline.* The central conferences, like other parts of Methodism, are subject to the General Conference.

The annual conferences comprising the central conferences send delegates to the General Conference. These persons participate fully in its deliberations, having both voice and vote. The presence of delegates from the central conferences at the General Conference is clear evidence of the global nature of the United Methodist Church.

THE JUDICIAL COUNCIL

The Judicial Council is not a conference in the sense of those discussed in this chapter, but it is a body that makes decisions affecting the entire denomination. When the three branches of Methodism united in 1939, this council was created in order to have a body that could determine the constitutionality of acts of the General Conference. In every organization there needs to be a method of resolving disputes and different interpretations of law. For United Methodism, the Judicial Council performs this function.

Composition

The Judicial Council consists of nine persons who are elected by the General Conference upon nomination by the Council of Bishops. The bishops nominate three times the number of vacancies, and nominations may be made from the floor. A system has been devised so that the composition of the Judicial Council will alternate, at one time having five clergy and four laypersons and, the next time, having four clergy and five laypersons.

Members are elected to eight-year terms and serve without pay. To preserve the independence of the Judicial Council, members cannot be members of the General Conference, any jurisdictional conference or general or jurisdictional board, or in administrative service in any connectional office. Alternate members are elected to insure that persons are available to serve if a vacancy occurs between sessions of the General Conference.

Functions

While the Judicial Council is often compared to the United States Supreme Court, Bishop Jack M. Tuell points out that there are some significant differences. The council does interpret the law and has the authority to declare legislation unconstitutional, but it does not receive cases in the same manner. While the Supreme Court hears cases that come from the lower courts, only a very small proportion of the council's work deals with appeals of decisions made by other bodies. The great proportion of its work is deciding matters of law and constitutionality that are brought by the several groups authorized to do so. The Judicial Council is "almost more like an administrative tribunal than it is a court as that term is used in civil law."[4]

The Judicial Council determines the constitutionality of any act of the General Conference upon appeal of a majority of the Council of Bishops or one-fifth of the members of the General Conference. It has the authority to determine the constitutionality of proposed legislation. Such an action is called a "Declaratory Decision." The Judicial Council will be present during the sessions of the General Conference and make several such decisions while the meeting is in progress.

Only certain groups are authorized to bring matters before the Judicial Council. These include the bishops, the general, jurisdictional, and annual conferences, and general and jurisdictional boards on matters relating to the work of or affecting the boards.

The Judicial Council hears and determines any appeal from a bishop's decision on a question of law made in an annual conference when requested by one-fifth of the members. It passes on decisions of law made by bishops in annual conferences and determines the legality of actions by general and jurisdictional boards. Finally, the council has the power to review a decision of a Committee on Appeals of a jurisdictional conference. It is to hear and determine the questions of law involved.

When the council declares any act of the General Conference unconstitutional and thus invalid, it is required to report the decision immediately to the General Conference. The decisions are final; there is no appeal.

The Judicial Council has provided an important service to the church. It has ruled on the constitutionality of General Conference actions. It has resolved conflicts. Many of its decisions have had a broad impact on the life and work of Methodism.

NOTES

1. *The Book of Discipline of The United Methodist Church, 1984* (Nashville: United Methodist Church Publishing House, 1984), para. 15.

2. Ibid., para. 610.

3. *The Book of Resolutions of The United Methodist Church, 1980* contains 218 pages of resolutions on 84 different subjects. After the 1984 General Conference, all the nonduplicating resolutions passed in the period 1968–1984 were published. There were positions taken on 145 different subjects by the six General Conferences that met during that span of time.

4. Jack M. Tuell, *The Organization of The United Methodist Church* (Nashville: Abingdon Press, 1985), p. 154.

Chapter 8

The Annual Conference

No organization has played a more significant role or has been more basic to the development and functioning of American Methodism than the annual conference. The constitution states, "The Annual Conference is the basic body of the Church."[1] It is not incorrect to describe United Methodism as a confederation of annual conferences, for it is these bodies that make many of the decisions affecting the life and work of both the local churches and the ministers.

For Methodism, the conference was and continues to be the method by which the mission of the church is determined and implemented. The delegates gather to decide together the specific tasks to which God is calling the church at a particular time. The theological understandings and the proposals for specific programs are subject to review by the body. When decisions are made, all are expected to honor them. A United Methodist conference is, therefore, a group of clergy and laypersons who by their membership in the body have covenanted to seek to determine the mission of the church and to find ways to carry out this mission. This is a reflection of Wesley's theology of grace as expressed in the fifth Instituted Means of Grace, Christian Conference.

As we have related, the church was organized in America by the ministers in a conference. At first there was only one conference, to which all clergy belonged. With church growth it was necessary to form regional conferences that met annually. A meeting of all the ministers was held only every four years. Further, rapid growth soon made it impossible for all the ministers to meet, so annual conferences, geographically defined, were organized in which all clergy were members. There also developed a churchwide quadrennial General Conference to which annual conferences sent delegates, a practice that continues today.

MEMBERSHIP

Annual conferences at first comprised only members of the clergy. Eventually laymen were admitted to that body and finally laywomen. Today the annual conference comprises two groups of delegates. The first is ministerial members, who include those in full connection, probationary members, associate members, and local pastors under full-time appointment to a pastoral charge. Probationary members, associate members, and full-time local pastors may not vote on constitutional amendments, election of general and jurisdictional conference delegates, or matters relating to the character and ordination of the clergy.

The second group constituting the annual conference is the lay delegates. These persons are elected by their charge conferences. They must have been members of the United Methodist Church for two years and active participants for four immediately preceding their election. The presidents of the annual conference's United Methodist Women, United Methodist Men, and the youth organization are lay delegates.

In addition, two persons under twenty-five years of age from each district are elected to membership in the annual conference. Part-time local and student pastors, lay missionaries appointed by the Board of Global Ministries serving outside the United States, and diaconal ministers serving within the bounds of the conference are seated and have the privilege of the floor without vote.

The Discipline requires that the number of lay and clergy members be equal. Because some annual conferences have a large number of retired ministers and those appointed beyond the local church (such as chaplains, teachers, or ministers to students), it is necessary to elect more lay delegates than there are pastoral charges. A common practice is for congregations of a certain membership to be permitted to elect two or three lay delegates.

Because an annual conference will generally meet for four or five days, it is sometimes difficult for congregations to find persons who are free to serve. The ability to participate in an extended meeting is often one criterion of a local church for election as a delegate to the annual conference.

Clergy in active service are expected to attend annual conferences. Persons who do not are required to report their reasons by letter. If an individual fails to do so, the conference secretary is required to report the matter to the Board of Ordained Ministry, presumably for disciplinary action.

NUMBER OF ANNUAL CONFERENCES

The number of annual conferences has been decreasing. In 1960 the total was 100. Of these, 17 were all-black annual conferences that made up the Central Jurisdiction. The merger with the Evangelical United Brethren resulted in the United Methodist Church in 1969 having 114 annual conferences, including 31 former E.U.B. and 10 black annual conferences (seven black conferences having already united with white conferences). Mergers during the next fifteen years reduced the total to the present 74.

A motivation for merger is to make the annual conference

boundaries coincide with the state boundaries. This has been attained to some degree, but because the distribution of United Methodists is uneven, many annual conferences encompass more than one state. Advocates of merger include persons who perceive a larger organization as being more efficient, clergy who see greater career opportunities, and bishops who would prefer to deal with only one annual conference. Whether this trend to larger conferences will continue is uncertain. Two recent merger proposals were defeated by vote of the conferences involved.

Annual conferences now meet during May or June. Some previously met in the fall, but this practice was discontinued in the late 1950s and early 1960s. One reason for the change was to permit clergy to move during the summer vacation period, making it easier for children to change schools.

THE ANNUAL SESSION

The most important event in the functioning of an annual conference is the yearly meeting. Almost all the ministerial members and an equal number of lay delegates will be present. The large number of delegates has limited the places where annual conferences can be held. In an earlier time it was the practice to meet in one of the churches, and local people often housed the delegates. The meeting place was changed from year to year, rotating among the larger churches. Today many conferences meet in college facilities or a civic center where there is a fieldhouse or auditorium large enough to accommodate the group. The bishop presides over sessions of the annual conference, which opens with the singing of Charles Wesley's hymn:

> And are we yet alive
> And see each other's face?
> Glory and thanks to Jesus give,
> For his almighty grace.[2]

Activities consist of worship, preaching, reports, and various kinds of business. There will be a memorial service for the ministers and spouses who have died during the year since the conference last met. The clergy will vote to admit candidates for the ministry into conference membership; this will be followed by a solemn ordination service.

The ministers must pass judgment on the character of all in their number. *The Discipline* gives the annual conference the power "to make inquiry into the moral and official conduct of its ministerial members."[3] The usual practice is for the district superintendent to report on all the preachers in the district, indicating that they are "blameless in their life and official administration," if such is the case.[4]

A "state of the conference" address is given by one of the district superintendents on behalf of all the members of that group. The conference boards and agencies make their reports. A representative of the denominational publishing house presents a check representing that conference's share of the year's profits that is to go toward ministers' pensions. The deans of theological seminaries in the region make reports, as do representatives of colleges, retirement homes, children's homes, and other church-related institutions.

The business of the conference includes setting the budget, acting on proposed programs, and dealing with resolutions on social and economic issues. The latter will state the annual conference's official position on some of the day's controversial issues. Some of these will be the subject of heated debate and the actions will be reported in the press, although the impact of such action may be negligible. Discussion of controversial resolutions sparks interest amid generally routine kinds of business.

The ministers tend to dominate the annual conference despite the fact that there are equal numbers of ministerial and lay delegates. The reason is that the clergy devote themselves full-time to the work of the church and tend to be more familiar with the issues before the body. They are more likely to be present, particularly when critical votes are to be taken. Furthermore, some laypersons are a bit reluctant to oppose the clergy, seeming to feel that the ministers probably know more about the matter in question.

The stationing of the ministers traditionally used to be a high point of the annual conference session. The bishop read the appointments as the concluding item of business. Some ministers learned only then of their reassignment. Appointments were actually being determined while the conference was in session, and their reading by the bishop brought the meeting to a dramatic conclusion.

Today decisions on appointments are made well before the conference meets. The required consultation between district superintendent, minister, and congregation makes this essential. Ministers arrive at the site of the annual conference knowing if and where they will be moving. Lay delegates have been informed who their pastor will be. The appointments are not officially set until the bishop announces them, so last-minute adjustments can still be made. Some bishops distribute printed lists of the appointments at the concluding sessions; others do so at the start of the conference. A few continue the tradition of actually reading the appointments of clergy. Whatever method is used, the decisions on appointments are now communicated to the interested parties apart from the annual conference session. This has reduced the suspense and eliminated a major source of drama previously associated with the gathering.

An annual conference will still have its exciting moments as a close vote decides a controversial issue. It will have its periods of dullness as an agency report drones on. It will have moments of humor as a clever speech is made. It will have its high periods as a gifted preacher moves the body or when, at the ordination service, a group of men and women dedicate their lives to the service of the church. The annual conference session is connectionalism in action as ministers and lay delegates meet to carry forward the work of Methodism within the geographical area of their responsibility.

ORGANIZATION

The Discipline mandates the organization that each annual conference is expected to have.[5] Some of these are essential for the conference to function, such as a treasurer's office to handle the funds and a Board of Ordained Ministry to screen candidates and deal with ministerial relations. There are conference organizations that parallel the national agencies; so each annual conference is required to have a Board of Global Ministries, a Board of Church and Society, a Commission on the Status and Role of Women, a Commission on Religion and Race, and so on.

These annual conference agencies serve as regional branch offices for the national agencies. Thus a general board will relate to and promote its program through the annual conference boards. Some general agencies also have parallel organizations in the churches, providing more direct contact between national and local levels. The Women's Division of the Board of Global Ministries relates to United Methodist Women's units in the jurisdictions, annual conferences, districts, and local churches. The result is an effective network that permits communication with all parts of the denomination for promoting programs and raising funds. The regional and local units serve as volunteer outlets for the programs and causes of the national agencies. The various parts of the denomination are thus organizationally connected.

A significant development in the way annual conference programs operate occurred with the establishment of the Council on Ministries in 1972. This came about as part of a general reorganization of the denominational bureaucracy which had among its goals a greater degree of coordination among boards and agencies. A major change for the annual conference lies in the way the staff members are employed and assigned. Previously the annual conference program staff were employed by and responsible to a specific board. Their work was restricted to that board—for example, Christian education, evangelism, or missions. Now the annual conference staff are employed by the Council on Ministries and are responsible for providing services to all the conference agencies. The theory is that the assignments will change and staff members will be deployed where they are most needed at a particular time. In practice, each staff member is assigned to several boards and agencies. This has resulted in the staff being spread so thin that the agencies do not feel that they are getting the services they need and the staff members feel frustrated because they have more responsibilities than they can fulfill well.

The Conference Council on Ministries has resulted in a layer of organization developing between the annual conference as a whole and the boards and agencies. It has made a coordinated conference program possible while downgrading somewhat the role of the boards and agencies. It has made the staff responsible for serving all the conference boards and agencies, not just the one that initially employed them. The staff have had to become more generalist than specialist. Whatever its advantages or disadvantages, the likelihood is that the council system will be part of the United Methodist structure indefinitely.

RELATIONSHIP WITH THE LOCAL CHURCH

The annual conference provides a basic link in the connectional system in that it connects a congregation with the rest of the denomination.

The local church's voice in denominational affairs is its delegate to the annual conference. While both the pastor and the layperson from the charge are delegates, the ministers tend to represent the perspective and interests of the clergy as a group. Therefore lay delegates have the burden of representing the viewpoint and concerns of the laity.

It should be noted that delegates are not instructed by their congregations to support or oppose specific items. The individuals are sent to the annual conference with the assumption that they will follow their conscience and act in the best interests of the church. They must come to their own decisions; they are not subject to any instructions from the group that elected them.

Decisions of the annual conference have a significant impact on the life of a congregation in several ways. The first lies in ministerial leadership. The clergy who are available for appointment to a church are members of the annual conference. Thus the bishop must select a pastor for a particular church from this group. The persons whom the clergy of the annual conference admit into ministerial membership determine who shall be the pastors of the churches.

The second impact is financial. While the local church sets the minister's salary, certain other costs of employing a pastor are determined by the annual conference. These include the minimum salary a minister must receive, whether the parsonage is furnished and the utilities paid, the policy regarding travel expenses, and the cost of medical and life insurance and pension. Besides determining these portions of the expenses pertaining to ministers, the annual conference requests a specific amount of money from each church to support the benevolent program and the administrative costs of the denomination and of the conference itself. The annual conference determines the formula by which the amount of each congregation's apportionments is set.

The third way in which the annual conference influences the local church is the development of conference programs. These are activities in which every congregation is expected to participate. It may be an evangelistic emphasis to secure new members or a program to help people deepen spiritual life. It may be a campaign to raise funds for the construction of new buildings. Not every congregation will participate in such programs, but a substantial proportion will.

The connection between the local church and the denomination is made specific by contacts with two persons, the district superintendent and the bishop. The district superintendent is the more important, because the contact is much more frequent. It is the district superintendent who presides over the annual charge conference, when many of the important local church decisions are made. These include such matters as election of the congregational officers, setting the budget, and buying or selling property. The bishop's appearances will be infrequent and usually limited to special events such as the dedication of a new building. Given the large number of churches in the episcopal area, many will never receive a visit from a bishop. This means that the district superintendent is the visible link between the local church and the annual conference, the person through which the congregation connects with the rest of the denomination.

THE MINISTER'S RELATIONSHIP WITH THE ANNUAL CONFERENCE

The United Methodist minister's primary relationship to the church is his or her membership in an annual conference. For the minister the annual conference has the characteristics of a church, an extended family, and a professional society. It is before a group of clergy that the candidate for the ministry must justify his or her call, and it is the same group that decides whether the call is valid.

The conference is the only "church" to which a minister belongs. When the individual is received into an annual conference, membership in a local church ceases. Most pastors will spend their lives serving congregations within the boundaries of one annual conference.

The annual conference is also like an extended family. The nature of the itinerant ministry tends to preclude the pastor from having long-term, close friends among the members of a parish. Therefore his or her closest friends are frequently other ministers. Often the friendships began in the denominational college or in theological seminary and continue throughout the person's lifetime. Spouses have tended to share in this kind of extended family. The term used to describe the nature of relationships among the ministerial members of an annual conference is "brotherhood."

Finally, the annual conference is a minister's professional society. It not only decides who shall be admitted into the ministry, but also maintains standards of conduct and performance. If a minister is to be disciplined or expelled from the profession, it is the ministerial members of the annual conference who must make the decision.

The trend is for annual conferences to move toward

being more of a professional society and less of an extended family or brotherhood. There are several reasons for this: (1) annual conferences are larger than they were even two decades ago, so a person gets to know a smaller proportion of the members; (2) more ministerial candidates are attending nondenominational colleges and seminaries, and (3) the increasing number of working spouses has made participation in conference activities less of a family affair.

A CRUCIAL ROLE

The annual conference is an institutional expression of the Methodist concept of a body that acts to carry on the work of the church under the guidance of the Holy Spirit. It acts on the assumption that God works through a group of dedicated Christian ministers and laypeople. It also assumes that the collective judgment is better than an individual's opinion.

It is not an exaggeration to say that the annual conference has been and continues to be the basic body of connectional Methodism. It is where the local church connects with the rest of the denomination. It is the context in which the clergy exercise their ministry, and it is the group to which they give the greatest loyalty. For the ministers and their families and, to a lesser degree, for the laity, the annual conference has provided a kind of Methodist Christian subculture. Sharing in the activities of the annual conference has helped give the Methodist people a sense of identity and common purpose.

Changes in the annual conferences will have a profound effect on the connectional system. If Methodism is to retain an effective connectionalism, the annual conference must continue to be an organization that laypersons trust as one which insures that their congregation will receive a competent and committed pastor. They must feel that the conference assists the local church in carrying out its task. The ministers must perceive the annual conference as the group which insures that only those worthy of their high calling are permitted to exercise their ministry under the authority of the United Methodist Church.

NOTES

1. *The Book of Discipline of The United Methodist Church, 1984* (Nashville: United Methodist Publishing House, 1984), para. 36.

2. *The Methodist Hymnal* (Nashville: United Methodist Publishing House, 1966), p. 336.

3. *The Discipline, 1984,* para. 703.4.

4. Ibid., para. 704.6.

5. Ibid., para. 706–743.

Chapter 9

The Local Church

The local congregation is the basic unit in the church. Within the context of the local church and the community in which it is located the Christian faith is manifest. It is where people hear the gospel preached, where they come to an understanding of the faith, and where they become—or fail to become—Christians. The local church provides the people who give leadership to and funds to support all other organizations and programs in the denomination. This has been the case throughout Christian history. The parish church has been one of society's most enduring institutions. It has continued virtually unchanged for two thousand years, and its prospects for the future remain unchanged.

The Discipline defines the local church as

> A community of true believers under the Lordship of Christ. It is the redemptive fellowship in which the Word of God is

> preached by persons divinely called, and the Sacraments are duly administered according to Christ's own appointment.[1]

It is also stated that the local church is a connectional society. The people have professed their faith in Christ, have been baptized, and have taken the membership vows and are therefore a part of a local congregation. As part of the United Methodist Church they are subject to its discipline. They are also part of the church universal which, as expressed in the Apostles' Creed, is "the holy catholic church."

NUMBER OF CHURCHES

The United Methodist Church in 1985 had 37,988 organized churches in the United States and Puerto Rico.[2] An organized church is a congregation that has a membership, officers, and a pastor appointed by the bishop. It has a building or, if a new church, is in the process of securing one. In addition there were 4,224 organized churches in the seven central conferences outside the United States. Data were also available from nineteen of the twenty-six affiliated autonomous Methodist church bodies overseas, reporting 7,828 congregations and 96,901 members.[3]

The United Methodist Church, like most Protestant denominations, has a large proportion of churches of small membership. More than two churches in five (42.2 percent) have fewer than a hundred members. Almost two-thirds (65.1 percent) of the congregations have fewer than two hundred members.

At the beginning of 1985 there were 25,727 pastoral charges—that is, one or more churches to which a minister was appointed—a figure representing slightly more than two-thirds (67.6 percent) of the organized churches. Thus, almost two-thirds of United Methodist churches are on a circuit, which means that they share their pastor with at least one other congregation. The practice of assigning a pastor to supervise several congregations has been a part of Methodist tradition from its beginning. The early circuit riders often covered a wide area and a large number of churches; today's circuit pastors tend to serve two-to-four congregations.

The circuit is facilitated by the Methodist system of placing ministers. The bishop appoints the pastors and decides which church(es) he or she will serve; thus he determines the congregations that will be on a circuit. The congregations are to be consulted, but the appointment is made by the bishop. The churches involved do not negotiate with each other to determine whether they will share a minister; the circuit system would probably be inoperable if the congregations had to reach consensus on selecting a pastor. The churches on a circuit must come to an agreement on such matters as each congregation's share of the minister's salary, the arrangement for the parsonage, and the schedule of worship services.

MEMBERSHIP

The Discipline states that "all persons seeking to be saved from their sins and sincerely desiring to be Christian in faith and practice are proper candidates for full membership in The United Methodist Church."[4] The church is inclusive and open to all persons without regard to race, color, national origin, or economic condition.

A candidate for membership must have been baptized in a United Methodist or in some other Christian church. Persons take four vows in making a profession of faith when they join a church:

1. To confess Jesus Christ as Lord and Savior and pledge their allegiance to his kingdom,
2. To receive and profess the Christian faith as contained in the Scriptures of the Old and New Testament,
3. To promise according to the grace given them to live a Christian life and always remain faithful members of Christ's holy Church,
4. And to be loyal to The United Methodist Church and uphold it by their prayers, their presence, their gifts and their service.[5]

In addition to making a profession of faith in this way, a person may transfer membership from a congregation of another denomination.

The pastor makes the decision as to who shall be received into membership. The pastor is also responsible for instructing prospective members on the meaning of the Christian faith and the history, organization, and teachings of the United Methodist Church. This includes conducting a confirmation class for youth.

The pastor is given explicit instructions regarding the relationship of children to the church. These include urging that parents present their children to the Lord at an early age in baptism and keeping an accurate register of all who have been baptized. The minister is also responsible for maintaining a "preparatory" membership roll that contains the names of all baptized children. Persons remain on this roll until they become full members or until they reach the age of nineteen, at which time they are transferred to a "constituency" roll. The preparatory membership roll is a tangible way for a congregation to express its responsibility to its children.

The United Methodist Church takes membership seriously. It is perceived as the most important commitment an individual can make. Therefore the church is reluctant to terminate the membership of people who are no longer active or who have moved away. The congregation is instructed to attempt to restore such persons to active participation or to persuade them to transfer to a church in the community where they currently reside. If these efforts prove unsuccessful over a three-year period, the person can be removed from the church roll by action of the charge conference.

ORGANIZATION

The form of organization that every local United Methodist Church is required to follow is determined by the General Conference and set forth in *The Discipline*. This includes the officers required of each congregation, the method by which they are elected, and their areas of responsibility. Also clearly spelled out are the several governing and program committees each congregation must have.

The Charge Conference

The most important meeting in the local church is the annual charge conference. This is the yearly business meeting at which the basic decisions affecting the life and ministry of the congregation for the coming year are made. It is also the meeting that relates the local church to the connection.

The present form of the charge conference has developed out of quarterly conferences. These were the four visits that the presiding elder (later, the district superintendent) made to each pastoral charge. The fourth quarterly conference was for electing officers, setting a budget, and tending to other business. In time, the district superintendent reduced the number of visits to two a year, so only the first and fourth quarterly conferences were held. Finally this was reduced to one and the name changed to "charge conference."

The district superintendent presides over the charge conference, which comprises certain designated local church officials and the pastor. In keeping with Methodist practice this is a delegated body with the members authorized to act on behalf of the congregation. The members present at any duly announced meeting constitute a quorum; therefore action cannot be blocked by recalcitrant members refusing to attend. The charge conference receives reports from the pastor and various organizations, evaluates the mission and ministry of the church, and adopts goals for the coming year. It recommends candidates for the ordained ministry and affirms the good standing in the congregation of persons seeking to become diaconal ministers. It elects the officers, sets the pastor's salary, authorizes the purchase or sale of property, and sets policies for the charge. It removes inactive members from the church rolls. It may recommend the return or the reassignment of the minister.

With the approval of the district superintendent, a congregation may have a "church conference," at which all members can vote on an issue that could otherwise be handled by the charge conference. This procedure is used when congregational consensus is required on some matter such as a proposal to erect a new building.

Although all church members may attend the charge conference, few persons other than the officers who are able to vote generally do so. Unless there is an unusual or controversial issue, most charge conferences tend to be perfunctory. Nevertheless, the charge conferences is a vital link in the connectional system. The district superintendent, who represents the denomination, is present. The local church leaders have the opportunity to hear from a denomination official and to express their views about issues beyond the local church. The charge conference should be a mechanism by which the local congregation and the denomination work together to achieve the goals of the church in both the local community and the larger society.

Trustees

Every local church must have a board of trustees consisting of not fewer than three or more than nine members. These persons must be of legal age as defined by the state. At least two-thirds must be members of the United Methodist Church. A reason for having non-Methodists on the board of trustees is that some churches have cemeteries which serve the entire community. Because these cemeteries are managed by the trustees, it is appropriate for a person from the community to sit on the board. The trustees are divided into classes, with one-third of the positions being filled every year by election to a three-year term.

The board of trustees is responsible for the church property, including overseeing maintenance and repair, buying and selling property, erecting buildings, and securing adequate insurance. The charge conference, however, has the authority to direct the board of trustees on matters related to church property and makes the final decision concerning purchase and sale.

Administrative Committees

The Discipline requires each local church to have three administrative committees. Each performs functions essential to the congregation.

The first is a committee on nominations and personnel comprising not more than nine persons besides the pastor, who is the chairperson. The committee is divided into classes with one-third being elected each year. The members are elected by the charge conference on nomination from the floor. The task of this committee is to nominate persons to serve in the various offices. A slate is presented to the charge conference. Other persons may be nominated from the floor, but most persons named by the committee get elected. The work of the committee is extremely important because it selects the laypersons who will lead the congregation.

The second is the committee on pastor-parish relations, having not fewer than five nor more than nine members. It represents the entire charge and must have at least one member from each church on a circuit. This committee is to meet at least quarterly. It consults with the pastor and staff concerning their relationship with the congregation. It interprets the need and expectations of the congregation to the minister. It is the group that the pastor uses to interpret his or her ministry to the congregation. It is the personnel committee with responsibility for the employed staff. This group also confers with the district superintendent regarding any reappointment or change of pastors.

The third is the committee on finance, which has been given the responsibility for developing the annual budget. The budget is submitted to the Administrative Board for review and adoption. This committee also has the task of developing and implementing plans to raise the income needed to meet the budget.

Administration and Program

The body responsible for the week-to-week governing of the local church is the Administrative Board, comprising the officers of the church. Quarterly meetings are required. The board is the executive agency of the charge conference and has general oversight of the administration and program of the local church. The pastor is the administrative officer. *The Discipline* states that the administrative board shall "initiate planning, establish objectives, adopt goals, authorize action, determine policy, evaluate the church's ministries, and review the mission and ministry of the church."[6]

A second group, the Council on Ministries, has been given the responsibility for developing and coordinating goals and program proposals. This body is to develop the program and present it to the administrative board. The situation is complicated by the fact that a number of people may serve on both bodies.

Each local church is required to have ten work areas to which a particular part of the program has been assigned:

(1) Christian Unity and Interreligious Concerns
(2) Church and Society
(3) Education
(4) Evangelism
(5) Higher Education and Campus Ministry
(6) Missions
(7) Religion and Race
(8) Status and Role of Women
(9) Stewardship
(10) Worship

Each work area is to develop programs using material provided by the general boards and agencies. Each is to keep the Council on Ministries aware of the needs and programs that have been developed to meet these needs.

Besides these, every congregation is to have four age-level and family coordinators. These persons are to work in the whole range of programs for their respective groups:

(1) Children's Ministries
(2) Youth Ministries
(3) Adult Ministries
(4) Family Ministries

The Discipline requires certain other organizations of every church, including the church school and the United Methodist Women. Some others are recommended, but not required, such as United Methodist Men, a Wills Task Force, a Health and Welfare Ministries representative, and a coordinator of communications. Provision is made for forming ad hoc task forces to deal with special matters as needed.

Options for the Small Church

The 1980 General Conference recognized that a majority of congregations are too small to have the required administrative board, council on ministries, ten work areas, and four age-level and family coordinators. It provided that the administrative board and council on ministries may be combined to form an Administrative Council. This body is to plan and implement the programs of nurture and outreach and have responsibility for the administration of the local church.

The work areas may be combined and reduced to two under the administrative council. The first is nurture and membership care and includes education, worship, and stewardship. The second is outreach and includes social concerns, religion and race, and evangelism. The four age-level and family coordinators are combined into one office.

By providing an alternate structure for the church of small membership, the General Conference recognized what was going on at the local level. Small churches simply could not accommodate the required structure, so they were informally adopting a simplified one. *The Discipline* now legitimizes what had been taking place unofficially.

PROPERTY

The Discipline requires that the titles to all property held by the church—including the general, jurisdictional, and annual conferences and the local churches—be held in trust for the United Methodist Church. Every deed is required to contain the following clause:

> In trust, that said premises shall be used, kept and maintained as a place of divine worship of The United Methodist ministry and members of The United Methodist Church; subject to the Discipline, usage and ministerial appointments of said church as from time to time authorized and declared by the General Conference and by the annual conference within whose bounds the said premises are situated. This provision is solely for the benefit of the grantee, and the grantor reserves no right or interest in said premises.[7]

A similar clause applies to the deeds of parsonages and any other property the church may require.

The "trust clause" ensures that the property will be retained for the use originally intended, that is, as a United Methodist place of worship and ministry. The persons who erect and pay for a United Methodist church building can be assured that the facility will continue to be used for its original purpose even after they are no longer on the scene.

A particular congregation cannot simply by majority vote withdraw from the denomination and retain the church property. Members can, of course, withdraw as individuals, but the property remains with those who continue as United Methodists. Should all the members leave, the building would revert to the annual conference, which would formally declare the church "abandoned" and determine what should be done with it. This happens occasionally in rural areas of declining population when a congregation ceases to exist.

During the civil rights struggles of the 1960s, some state legislatures enacted laws allowing congregations to vote to withdraw from the denomination and retain the property. The Methodist Church in Union Springs, Alabama, subsequently took that action.[8] The congregation became independent, severed all ties with the denomination, and retained control of the church building. Bishop W. Kenneth Goodson of the Birmingham area then brought suit on behalf of the loyal minority, claiming that they were the Methodist congregation and that the dissident group was holding the property illegally. The litigation lasted seven years. The Supreme Court of the State of Alabama finally ruled unanimously that the trust clause was valid and ordered the dissident congregation to turn over the keys to the property to Bishop Goodson. The trust clause has been tested in other legal cases and has been upheld.

It is possible, of course, for a church to dispose of property. This requires the signature of the pastor and the district superintendent. *The Discipline* requires that such action be taken only after an investigation to ensure that it will be in the best interests of the ministry of that church and of other United Methodist congregations in the vicinity.

The trust clause is a significant aspect of connectionalism. It reminds local churches that they are part of a larger group to whom they have a responsibility and are accountable. It ensures that property set aside by Methodist people for worship and ministry will continue to be used for that purpose as long as it is needed in the community.

NOTES

1. *The Book of Discipline of The United Methodist Church, 1984* (Nashville: United Methodist Publishing House, 1984), para. 201.
2. *1985 General Minutes of the Annual Conferences of The United Methodist Church* (Evanston, Ill.: General Council on Finance and Administration, 1985), p. 29.
3. Ibid., pp. 26–27.
4. *The Discipline, 1984,* para. 216.
5. Ibid., para. 211.
6. Ibid., para. 256.
7. Ibid., para. 2503.
8. In 1964 the Alabama State Legislature passed the Dumas Act, which allowed any congregation on any Sunday to withdraw from the denomination by a two-thirds vote of the members present and to retain the church property.

Chapter 10

The Superintendency

Since its very beginning, the Methodist Church has had an office of superintendent. This includes the general superintendent, or bishop, and the district superintendent. These officials have occupied a key role in the connectional system. The bishops, having authority to appoint ministers, may be the most powerful church officials in American Protestantism. The district superintendents derive much of their power from the bishops. The way Methodists define these offices reflects their understanding of the church and determines to a great degree how the denomination functions.

THE BISHOP

The bishop has been a key figure in American Methodism since the denomination was organized in 1784. The name the assembly selected, "The Methodist Episcopal Church," made it immediately clear what form of government the new denomination was to have. The election of Francis Asbury to the office gave the church a man of strong will and long tenure who in his lifetime ensured that the bishop would be a powerful official.

The General Conference of 1808 took action that firmly established the office of bishop. It placed in the constitution six items that became known as "the Restrictive Rules," one of which states:

> The General Conference shall not change or alter any part or rule of our government so as to do away with episcopacy or destroy the plan of our itinerant general superintendency.[1]

A powerful episcopacy will inevitably be the subject of controversy. Throughout their history Methodists have debated the role of the bishop. This early on resulted in schism, for in 1792 James O'Kelly and a group of ministers withdrew to form a rival denomination when the conference refused to provide a method by which a minister could appeal his appointment. This issue also lay at the source of the schism that resulted in the formation of the Methodist Protestant Church in 1830. The authority of the General Conference to order a bishop to cease to function was foremost in the debate that caused Methodism to split into northern and southern churches in 1844.

The controversy has continued with varying degrees of intensity to the present. The serious attempt in 1976 to change the life tenure of bishops to a limited term is a recent example. The bishop has been a significant and unique part of Methodism since its beginning in America. The office and the debate over its proper role can be expected to continue.

Bishop, or General Superintendent

Methodism has combined into one office the positions of bishop and general superintendent. It may be argued that the church is not sure whether it wants a bishop or a general superintendent. Actually it wants (and probably needs) both. *The Discipline* defines the nature of the superintendency:

> The task of superintending The United Methodist Church resides in the office of bishop and extends to the district superintendent, with each possessing distinct responsibilities. From apostolic times, certain ordained persons have been entrusted with the particular task of superintending. Those who superintend carry responsibility for ordering the life of the church.[2]

Bishops are selected from the group of elders who have been ordained to the ministry of Word, Sacrament, and Order. The bishops are chosen for a specific task, but continue to share in the full ministry as ordained elders. Elders are consecrated as bishops, not ordained to that office. Although much is made of the fact that the bishop remains an elder and is not a third order, the church treats the position as if it were. Bishops are elected for life and are treated almost as if they were not just set apart, but set above the other clergy.

Three key words in the Restrictive Rules define the role of the bishop: "itinerant general superintendent." Bishops were at first itinerants and as such were expected to travel throughout the connection. They were not to be diocesan bishops with authority limited to a specific geographical area. So the early bishops traveled through the entire church to supervise the work and preside over the annual conferences.

The second word, "general," gives the bishops responsibility for a wide range of church activities. The authority is not restricted to the episcopal task, but is broadly defined to include the entire denomination. The bishops are to "Lead and oversee the spiritual and temporal affairs of The United Methodist Church."[3]

The third word is "superintendent." Methodist bishops are given the responsibility of overseeing the work of the church. The primary task of the bishops is administrative, not sacramental. He or she will operate out of an office located either in a downtown commercial building or a church-owned office building somewhere in a metropolitan area. Except for the decorations, the office could not be distinguished from that of any corporation executive. The setting itself illustrates that the bishops administer a geographical area and superintend the work of the church.

The bishops are responsible to perform certain rites. These include the consecration of bishops, the ordination of deacons and elders, and the commissioning of diaconal ministers and home missionaries. Only a bishop can ordain ministers. The bishops also dedicate church buildings as time permits.

The office of bishop has gained increasing symbolic value over the years. It is perceived as having great prestige. The occupants are expected to possess both spiritual depth and political acumen. Their support is constantly sought for a variety of causes. A meeting is considered more significant if the bishop attends. Stories, some undoubtedly embellished, are circulated about the more colorful bishops.

In summary, the United Methodist Church has an office of itinerant general superintendent who is also expected to be a spiritual leader. It should not be surprising that this results in some ambivalence about the bishops' role.

Election

Since the unification of 1939, bishops have been elected by the jurisdictions. They serve within the jurisdiction that elects them. Although a constitutional amendment was approved in the early 1970s that makes it possible for a bishop to be transferred from one jurisdiction to another, no transfer has yet occurred.

The number of bishops to which a jurisdiction is entitled is determined by a formula that takes into account the number of its church members and its geographical size. However, each jurisdiction is entitled to a minimum of six. Currently there are forty-six active bishops in the United States.

There are no formal nominations of persons for the office of bishop at the jurisdictional conference. Delegates may vote for any elder in the church. The first few ballots show who is receiving support and thus serve as an informal nominating process. Although the episcopacy is not limited to elders who are members of the annual conferences within the jurisdiction, the election of someone from a different jurisdiction is extremely rare.[4]

The Discipline recommends, but does not require, that a plurality of 60 percent of the jurisdictional delegates be required for an episcopal election. Because the jurisdictional conferences vary in size, the number of votes needed to elect a bishop also varies. For example, it requires more than three times as many votes to elect someone to the episcopacy in the Southeastern Jurisdiction than in the Western.

A trend has developed over the past two decades of people actively seeking the episcopacy. Twenty years ago, the individual who openly campaigned for election would receive little or no support. Someone who openly expressed ambition for the office was certain not to be chosen. This did not, however, prevent the person's friends from discreetly soliciting support.

The 1976 General Conference included in *The Discipline* a provision by which an annual conference at the regular session preceding the jurisdictional conference "may name one or more nominees for episcopal election."[5] The delegates to the jurisdictional conference may vote for any elder, not just those nominated. An annual conference cannot require any of its delegates to vote for a particular candidate.

The result of this process has been increasingly open campaigning by aspirants to episcopacy. Nominees sometimes meet with the annual conference delegates to the jurisdictional conference. A common practice now is the circulation of a brochure that contains the candidate's photograph, sometimes a picture of the entire family, and information promoting the candidate's qualifications for the episcopacy. Persons are now also endorsed by caucuses and special-interest groups. A national meeting of United Methodist clergywomen in February 1983 endorsed Leontine T. Kelly for the episcopacy. This group collected two thousand dollars to finance her campaign.

The selection of bishops has changed drastically from a system where the episcopacy was perceived to be the "call of the church" to one in which individuals openly campaign for the office. This system of overt campaigning will certainly have an effect on the office of bishop, but it is still too early to determine the nature and extent of the change.

Assignment

A Jurisdictional Committee on Episcopacy recommends the boundaries of the episcopal areas and the assignment of the bishops to their respective residences. The election of new bishops must have been completed and all consulted before the recommendations are made. The assignments are then made by the jurisdictional conference.

In the early days of Methodism a bishop resided wherever he chose. The bishops were expected to travel through the connection, so the residence for their families was left to their own judgment. The 1872 General Conference of the Methodist Episcopal Church elected eight bishops and recommended (but did not require) that they live in or near eight cities. It was not until 1900 that the General Conference took the next step of assigning the bishops to their residences. After unification in 1939, *The Discipline* simply stated, "Each Jurisdictional Conference may fix the Episcopal residences within its Jurisdiction and assign the Bishops to the same."[6]

The episcopal areas have tended to carry the name of the city in which the bishop lived, for example, Boston, Raleigh, or Houston. Some areas now carry the name of a state, such as Wisconsin or Tennessee-Virginia.

Bishops are assigned to an episcopal area for a term of four years. Until 1964 a bishop could be reassigned to the same area indefinitely. In that year a limit of twelve consecutive years in the same area was instituted. In 1976 the limit was reduced to eight years. However, a Jurisdictional Committee on Episcopacy may recommend by a two-thirds vote an additional four years if it "determines such an assignment to be in the best interest of the jurisdiction."[7]

Duties

The constitution provides that "the bishops shall have residential and presidential supervision in the Jurisdictional Conference in which they are elected or to which they are transferred."[8] The presidential duties include presiding in the general, jurisdictional, and annual conferences, forming the districts (after the number has been set by the annual conference), consecrating bishops, ordaining elders and deacons, consecrating diaconal ministers, and commissioning deaconesses and home missionaries.

The residential duties include making the appointments of the ministers in the annual conferences, determining which churches shall be stations and circuits, and setting the charge conference membership of ministers not serving in a local church. Bishops never become involved in another's area. In fact, one will not make an appearance in another area without an invitation from the resident bishop. Responsibilities outside their area involve matters related to the whole church, not to another bishop's area.

The Discipline assigns duties to the bishop that seem to be more formidable than the presidential and residential duties designated in the constitution. These are of two kinds: those that relate to the annual conferences within the episcopal area, and those that relate to the entire denomination. An examination of these two types of duties is necessary to understand the way the episcopacy really functions in the United Methodist Church. Moreover, they help to explain why a United Methodist bishop may be the most powerful denominational official in Protestantism.

There are two major sources of episcopal power. The first is lifetime tenure; a bishop's term does not expire. Barring resignation (which has occurred only three times in two hundred years) or removal for cause (which has never happened), the bishop fulfills his duties and is a person to be reckoned with until retirement. Even after retirement, the person remains a bishop and participates in both the College (jurisdictional) and Council (churchwide) of Bishops.

The second major source of power is the authority to appoint the pastors to their charges or other places of service. United Methodist bishops have their greatest authority within their areas. The bishop is the general superintendent who appoints all the pastors and is thus someone with whom the clergy and the congregations must reckon. While full members of the annual conference are guaranteed an appointment, the bishops decide what that appointment shall be. This includes where the minister shall live and what his or her salary will be. The bishop does not set the salary, but knows what salary a local church will pay. The United Methodist minister has no recourse against an arbitrary or vindictive appointment by a bishop; he or she must accept the appointment. The only available options are to resign from the ministry or to seek transfer to an annual conference in a different episcopal area.

Although a bishop has considerable power, certain factors inhibit its abuse and overly arbitrary use. The first is that persons elected to the episcopacy are clergy who have long served the church and are dedicated to its mission. They want their actions to enhance the church's witness and ministry. Second, the effectiveness of the bishops depends to a great degree on their ability to lead, to inspire confidence among the clergy and laity, and to convince them to give their time, talents, and resources to the church's task. While the bishops fix the appointments, their actions must make sense and be accepted by both clergy and congregations. Third, there is peer pressure as the bishops counsel with each other. All the bishops are aware that their actions are being monitored not only by the constituents in their areas but also by episcopal colleagues.

While the United Methodist bishops have considerable power in the episcopal areas to which they have been assigned, they are also general superintendents with responsibility for the entire church. In this capacity they are charged with the task of leading and overseeing the spiritual and temporal affairs of the church and guiding it in its mission of witness and service in the world. They are instructed to travel through the connection at large, to provide liaison in ecumenical activities and relationships, to organize such missions as the General Conference authorizes, and to promote the evangelistic witness of the church. However, this denomination-wide leadership is exercised through the Council of Bishops. *The Discipline* states:

> The Council of Bishops is thus the corporate expression of episcopal leadership in the Church and through the Church into the world. The Church expects the Council of Bishops to speak to the Church and from the Church to the world.[9]

The bishops speak to the church in two ways. First there is the Episcopal Address, given at the opening of every General Conference. This is a kind of "state of the church" report. It represents the collective sentiment of the bishops on the issues faced by the church and offers their counsel as to what should be done about them. Second, from time to time the Council of Bishops issues statements to the church.[10] These are infrequent; only twenty-two such messages were issued between 1939 and 1979. They have tended to be in response to some serious matter in the church or society such as support for private and parochial schools, racial tensions in the United States, and the war in Vietnam. These statements represent the thinking of the bishops on significant issues and give guidance to Methodist people on how they should respond.

The bishops have had substantial authority in the denomination as a whole, not because *The Discipline* gives them power to act, but because they have been recognized as the spiritual and temporal leaders of the church. The bishops are ministers who were selected for the office by the denominational leaders. They are persons who have been perceived as having such qualities as dedication to the church, spiritual depth, sensitivity and administrative ability. Traditionally, an individual is not expected to seek the office, but is considered called to it by the church. Thus the person elected to the episcopacy is already recognized as someone who possesses the necessary characteristics for the office. The churchwide authority of the United Methodist bishops, therefore, depends on the acceptance of the persons who hold the office as leaders of the church.

THE DISTRICT SUPERINTENDENT

The district superintendent is the person in the United Methodist connectional system who provides the most visible link between the local congregation and the rest of the denomination. He or she visits the local church regularly and presides over the annual charge conference at which many of the congregation's important decisions are made. The superintendent may represent the bishop in consulting with the minister and the lay members concerning the appointment of the pastor. Most districts are of a size that the superintendent is available to work with the minister and the congregation as circumstances require.

The selection of district superintendents is one of the most important decisions that bishops make, because they are naming close advisers. District superintendents counsel the bishop on a broad range of matters. With the bishop they make up the cabinet, which as a group considers all pastoral appointments. The cabinet is an inner circle of annual conference leaders that not only makes many important decisions but sets the tone of the conference.

Development of the Office

The office of the district superintendent evolved early in American Methodism because of certain obvious and pressing needs. The church was growing rapidly, and the number of trained and experienced ministers was few. The ordained elders were given oversight of a number of unordained and often poorly educated preachers, to guide and counsel them. They were to conduct the service of Holy Communion, which the unordained preachers could not do. Twelve of the twenty-five elders on the roll in 1785 were assigned this supervisory task. Each had from five to twenty preachers under this direction. These ordained ministers came to be known as "presiding elders," a term that continued in use until the twentieth century in both major branches of the church and in the southern church until unification in 1939.

Eventually the practice developed of appointing a presiding elder to a particular district. This is a group of churches in a geographical area. The districts continue to be the major divisions within an annual conference. The conference itself determines how many districts there will be. The bishop then decides which churches will be in a district and sets the boundaries. At the end of 1985 there were 537 districts in the United States and Puerto Rico. This figure has changed little during recent years; a decade earlier the total was 549, a difference of only 12.

The size of a district will depend on such factors as the concentration of the Methodist membership, the number of churches, and the number of pastoral charges. Most districts will have from forty to sixty pastoral charges and from forty to a hundred local churches. Some districts are concentrated in a metropolitan area where no church is further than a forty-five minute drive from the district parsonage; others are large, such as the one that encompasses a third of North Dakota.

The trend in recent years to place restrictions on church officials has included the district superintendent. At first a minister could serve indefinitely. Some persons were presiding elders for most of their careers. After the merger of the three branches of Methodism in 1939, the district superintendents were permitted to serve a maximum of six consecutive years. However, after three years in a parish or other appointment, he could again be named district superintendent. Some persons served as many as four six-year terms.

Currently a minister may be appointed to a district for no more than six years in any consecutive nine. No one may serve as a district superintendent for a total of more than twelve years. In practice this usually means that a person may serve two six-year terms separated by an interval of at least three years, during which he or she serves as the pastor of a church or in some other type of appointment.

The power of the district superintendents derives in large part from their appointment by the bishop. They serve at the pleasure of the bishop; indeed, to a great degree they represent an extension of the office of the bishop.

In one sense the district superintendents are between the bishop and the ministers. They are elders who have served appointments in the annual conference. They will usually return to a local church when their term is over. They represent the interests of the clergy to the bishops, but they are accountable to the bishop, not to their cleric peers.

A point of controversy from time to time has been whether the district superintendents should be elected by the ministers or appointed by the bishop. This matter surfaced early when the 1820 General Conference took action to enable the elders to select seven candidates for presiding elder from among whom the bishop would have been required to make the final selection. Bishop-elect Joshua Soule refused to be consecrated because he felt strongly that such an action was unconstitutional and in violation of the third Restrictive Rule, which states that the church may not do away with the episcopacy (and which Soule had written earlier). The matter was postponed for a quadrennium, when the proposal was dropped (thus permitting Soule to be elected bishop again and this time consecrated to the office).

The appointment of district superintendents by the bishop seems to be a permanent part of United Methodism. The Evangelical United Brethren Church followed the practice of electing conference superintendents; there was no limit on tenure, so some persons served for many years. At the merger in 1968 the Methodist model of an appointed district superintendent was followed.

One bishop may view the district superintendency quite differently from another. One may expect his or her superintendents to clear all decisions and to operate a program that is coordinated with that of the annual conference. Another may allow or even encourage a high degree of freedom in the districts. The style and ground rules are set by the bishop.

The office of the bishop would function quite differently

if the district superintendents were elected by the clergy. There could be an open adversarial relationship between the bishop and the district superintendents, something which is not now possible. In a particularly tense situation in an annual conference during the 1960s, one bishop commented to the author, "My superintendents know that they have to be loyal to me and to the stand of the church or they will be out of the cabinet this afternoon."

Duties

The Discipline lists more than three pages of duties for district superintendents.[11] These are grouped into five categories. The first is supervising the pastors and churches in the district. This is the traditional role of the presiding elder, who in times past was overseer of Methodist work in a geographical area. Today the responsibilities include helping congregations formulate a statement of purpose, helping pastors to determine priorities, observing all aspects of the local church's ministry, and working with the pastor-parish relations committees.

The second duty involves personnel, which includes ministerial recruitment. It requires working with the District Committee on Ordained Ministry in examining candidates for the clergy and building a relationship with them. Personnel responsibilities encompass developing adequate salary support and benefits for the clergy and working with the bishop and cabinet before appointments are made.

The third responsibility is pastoral. This means giving pastoral support and care to ministers and their families, a function often described as being "pastor to pastors." While superintendents may be experienced and skilled ministers, it is often difficult for them to counsel the ministers about either professional or personal problems. The issue is role conflict: it is virtually impossible to be a pastor and a supervisor at the same time. Because superintendents have a voice in ministerial appointments, a pastor will be reluctant to share a problem if that knowledge may hinder his or her career later.

The fourth duty is administration, which includes presiding at the charge conferences, working with local churches regarding matters of property, and promoting financial support for local church and denominational causes. The district office is also required to keep records of abandoned church properties and cemeteries and of any endowments or trust funds belonging to churches on the district.

The fifth task is to administer the programs of the denomination within the bounds of the district. The superintendent serves as the executive officer of the District Council on Ministries and as a member of the Annual Conference Council on Ministries. In these roles it is the superintendent's responsibility to see that the churches of the district participate in and support the various programs of the annual conference and the denomination.

Despite the long list of duties which *The Discipline* assigns to the district superintendent, the position is not clearly defined. This is shown in two studies of the office.[12] Given such a wide range of responsibilities, the superintendent is forced to establish priorities as to which will receive time and energy. Murray H. Leiffer says of the demands of the superintendent:

> The superintendency has never benefited by even a relatively precise job definition. It was established as an extension of the bishop's arm. With the passage of time certain duties were specified in legislation for this executive assistant. Their number and variety have steadily increased and others . . . have been informally attached to the office. The result is an inchoate agglomeration of duties more or less consistent with the central function of administration.[13]

Supervision vs. Program

The trend in the past half-century has been for district superintendents to be more involved in denominational programming and less in supervising pastors and local churches. The change from holding four quarterly conferences to one annual charge conference is a sign of this trend.

District superintendents are now expected to promote the programs of the annual conference and the denominational boards and agencies. A quadrennial meeting of district superintendents is sponsored by the general church agencies to acquaint them with the various programs. The superintendents are correctly perceived as the critical link between the denominational organizations and the local congregation.

The result is that pressure has increased for the district superintendent to become a kind of local representative of the boards. Conference agencies want district superintendents on their boards of directors. Superintendents' time appears to be increasingly devoted to activities other than working with pastors and congregations on local concerns. The responsibility for supervision still resides in the office, and the superintendent must deal with problems in local churches; but the demand for leadership in promoting denominational programs will continue.

THE FUTURE OF THE SUPERINTENDENCY

Methodists have always been conscious of the power inherent in the office of the general superintendent, and there continues to be uneasiness about that power. The most serious controversies and schisms in the history of the denomination have involved the power of the bishops. There has been a long-term trend to increase the restrictions placed on both the bishops and the district superintendents. In the past quarter of a century, restrictions have included placing a limit on the time a bishop may serve in an episcopal area, first to twelve and subsequently to eight consecutive years, and lowering the retirement age so that a bishop must retire if he or she reaches age sixty-six prior to the jurisdictional conference. While an attempt to establish a "term episcopacy" and thus eliminate life tenure was defeated in 1976, it represented the most serious threat to the traditional episcopacy in Methodism's history.

Limitations placed on district superintendents include a lifetime limit of twelve years in the office, with each term no longer than six years and each term separated by an interval of at least three years. This restriction has eliminated those few career district superintendents who were continually reappointed after the required three years in another post. The feeling seems to be that certain people had too much power in an annual conference.

A new factor affecting how the superintendents function is the mandatory consultation regarding appointments. While the bishops still fix the appointments, the fact that they are now required to follow a process in appointment making that entails consultation with the minister and the pastor-parish relations committee is a further limitation on the bishops' and the district superintendents' power. *The Discipline* states that consultation is not merely notification or the selection of a minister by a committee, but "a continuing process and a more intense involvement during the period of change in appointment."[14] It is impossible for the bishops and district superintendents to be required to involve a number of persons in a decision without its having an influence on the decision and to some degree limiting their power.

There is a trend in American society for individuals to want more input into the decisions that affect their lives. The Methodist clergy, however, have traditionally been persons under orders, and the orders were given by the bishop. Now the consultation process has given both clergy and congregations a voice in the appointment process. It is unlikely that this will be reversed. The long-term result will be a significant change in the way bishops function in this matter and probably a lessening of the bishops' power.

Methodism has never had a ministry that was called by the congregation; ministers have been sent by the bishop. To a great degree the clergy have put their lives in the hands of the bishop. They have done so because they have had confidence that the bishop is a person of integrity who can be trusted to act under the guidance of the Holy Spirit in the best interest of the church. The minister who was required to make sacrifices or serve in a particularly difficult situation could feel that it was for a worthwhile purpose. Methodism requires a superintendency that is perceived to function in the best interests of the entire church if its authority is to be accepted.

Thus the superintendency has been a key part of the Methodist connectional system. The nature and function of these offices—general and district superintendent—have been critical to Methodism's self-understanding as a denomination. Any fundamental change in the church's theology or polity will involve the superintendency. The changes in the past two decades that have attempted on the one hand to maintain the power of the bishop and on the other hand to limit it reflect the lack of clarity and consensus about the office. Whatever course the United Methodist Church follows—whether it retains a strong episcopacy or moves in the direction of a presbyterian or congregational system—how we understand the nature and function of the superintendency will be at the heart of our theology and polity.

NOTES

1. *The Book of Discipline of The United Methodist Church, 1984* (Nashville: United Methodist Publishing House, 1984), para. 17.
2. Ibid., para. 501.
3. Ibid., para. 514.
4. Gerald H. Kennedy was elected a bishop by the Western Jurisdiction in 1948 when he was a pastor in Kansas, which is in the South Central Jurisdiction. However, most of his ministry had been in California, which is in the Western Jurisdiction. In 1984, Leontine T. Kelly, a black women who was a member of the Virginia Annual Conference, was elected by the Western Jurisdiction. At the time of her election she was serving on the staff of the Nashville-based General Board of Discipleship.
5. *The Book of Discipline of The United Methodist Church, 1976* (Nashville: United Methodist Publishing House, 1976), para. 506.
6. *Doctrines and Discipline of The Methodist Church, 1940* (Nashville: United Methodist Publishing House, 1940), para. 340.
7. *The Discipline, 1984,* para. 507.
8. Ibid., para. 52.
9. Ibid., para. 526.2.

10. *Messages of the Council of Bishops of The United Methodist Church, 1939–1979* (Office of the Secretary of the Council of Bishops of The United Methodist Church, 1979).

11. *The Discipline, 1984,* para. 517–524.

12. These studies were done by Murray H. Leiffer in 1960 and 1971. The findings were published in two volumes, *The Role of the District Superintendent in the Methodist Church* (Evanston, Ill.: Bureau of Social and Religious Research, 1960) and *The District Superintendent in the United Methodist Church* (Evanston, Ill.: Bureau of Social and Religious Research, 1971).

13. Leiffer, *The District Superintendent in the United Methodist Church,* p. 115.

14. *The Discipline, 1984,* para. 530.

Chapter 11

The General Boards and Agencies

The average United Methodist layperson and probably a large number of clergy do not understand the general boards and agencies. Everyone knows of their existence, a fact that is evident every year when the congregation prepares its annual budget and notes the amount of apportionments and other "askings." Many, if not most, United Methodists have only a vague idea of what the national agencies actually do, how they go about their jobs, and how they are managed.

There are several reasons why it is important for United Methodists to understand the general boards and agencies. First, these organizations expend a great deal of money. Most of the funds contributed to the benevolent programs of the denomination are channeled through one or more of the agencies that determine which programs shall and shall not receive support. Much of the support for institutions such as schools, colleges, seminaries, hospitals, and community centers are also funneled through these agencies. The control of funds gives the agencies a considerable degree of power in certain areas of the church.

Second, the national agencies control the channels of communication within the denomination. They produce the newspapers and magazines; they determine the content of the church school literature. These agencies are not only responsible for determining which matters are brought to the attention of the constituency, but they take positions on issues that they expect church members to accept.

Third, the general boards and agencies have a significant influence on the denomination's legislative process. Many persons are unaware of this. The staff members employed by the general agencies are full-time professionals who work on matters dealing with virtually every aspect of the church. A legislative proposal coming from a general agency is assured a hearing—and a better-than-average chance of passage—by the General Conference. The subjects with which the agencies deal and on which they may propose legislation cover virtually every aspect of the church and ministry.

AUTHORITY AND MANAGEMENT

The general boards and agencies owe their existence to the General Conference. Every four years this body passes legislation that authorizes the creation or continuation of the general agencies, defines their areas of responsibility, sets their structure, and determines the amount of funds they shall receive. Most general conferences make only minor changes in the church bureaucracy. Occasionally there are major changes in an agency, and there have been times when all the agencies have undergone drastic alterations. The term that has come to be used to signify change in the church bureaucracy is "restructure."

Because the authority for the general boards and agencies comes directly from the General Conference, there is a high level of anxiety among persons associated with these organizations as the quadrennium comes to an end. A great deal of time and energy goes into attempting to ensure that the General Conference will continue the various agencies and provide the needed funds.

While the authority and the funding are provided by the General Conference, some agencies have developed long traditions that give them a degree of permanence. The first missionary society, to which the Board of Global Ministries is the successor, was organized in 1819. It is difficult to imagine a denomination without some agency responsible for the mission program.

General church agencies over the years have acquired not only traditions, but also endowments, property, and obligations, all of which contribute to their permanence. Endowments are frequently designated for specific purposes such as mission work in a particular country. Property held by the general agencies may include the home office, retirement and children's homes, hospitals and clinics, and schools, either in the United States or abroad. Obligations encompass the pension claims of retired workers and the responsibility to use the endowment income consistent with the instructions of the donors.

Two categories of persons are responsible for the operation of general boards and agencies. The first category comprises the members of the boards of managers; the second is the staff.

The Board of Managers

Members of the board of managers of each agency are elected by the jurisdictional conferences. The number each jurisdiction may elect is determined by its numerical strength. The managers are elected for a term of four years and may serve a maximum of eight consecutive years.

The process of election to the boards of managers of the general agencies uses a quota system established in 1972. Each annual conference nominates at least fifteen people to a jurisdictional pool. Where possible, at least one, but not more than five, is to be included from each of seven categories: (1) clergy (including at least one woman), (2) laywomen, (3) laymen, (4) racial and minority persons (at least one Asian American, Black American, Hispanic American, and Native American), (5) youth, (6) young adults, and (7) persons with a handicapping condition. Whenever possible, one clergy, one laywoman, and one layman shall have been delegates to the previous General Conference.[1] From this pool of nominees the jurisdictional conference elects the members of the boards of managers of the general boards and agencies. In addition, a specific number of bishops are selected by the Council of Bishops to serve on each board.

The membership of each board must be one-third clergy (including at least one woman), one-third laymen, and one-third laywomen. Efforts should be made to include other categories of persons; it is recommended that 25 percent of the board members be ethnic and racial minority persons.

The responsibility for a particular agency rests with its board of managers. This is the body which sets policy, employs and directs the staff, prepares the budget and authorizes the expenditure of funds. The managers' responsibilities are similar to that of a board of directors of a corporation or a board of trustees of a college.

The Staff

The second category of persons who have responsibility for a general board or agency are the members of the staff. The board of managers selects the chief executive, who has the title of general secretary, and several other top executives. These persons are given the authority to employ other persons needed for the agency to operate. Quota systems have been established to ensure that women and members of ethnic and language minorities will be hired. For example, the General Board of Global Ministries requires that 40 percent of its senior executives be women.

The staffs of general boards and agencies range in size from a few employees to several hundred. Their headquarters are dispersed among five metropolitan areas: Chicago, Dayton, Nashville, New York, and Washington.

ORGANIZATION

The section of *The Discipline* dealing with the general agencies contains 116 pages. It is the longest chapter and makes up 15 percent of the entire volume. Several types of agencies are defined.[2]

1. *General Council*—an organization created to perform defined responsibilities of review and oversight on behalf of the General Conference in relation to other general agencies. Examples are the General Council on Ministries and the General Council on Finance and Administration.
2. *General Board*—a continuing body to carry out assigned functions of program, administration, and/or service. These are the General Board of Church and Society, the General Board of Discipleship, the General Board of Higher Education and Ministry, the General Board of Global Ministries, the General Board of Pensions, and the General Board of Publication.
3. *Standing General Commission*—an organization created to fulfill a specific function for an indefinite period of time. There are four standing general commissions: Archives and History, Christian Unity and Interreligious Concerns, Religion and Race, and Status and Role of Women.
4. *General Commission*—an organization created to fulfill a specific function for a limited period of time. The Commission on Central Conference Affairs is an example.

The Discipline divides the general agencies into two categories. The first category is program related and consists of the boards and commissions that have program or advocacy functions such as the Board of Church and Society or the Commission on Religion and Race. The second category comprises agencies that have primarily administrative or service functions; examples are the Board of Pensions and the Commission on Archives and History.

While *The Discipline* defines the types of agencies, the

fact is that they only fit the categories in a very general way. What a particular agency actually does is the result of not only the task assigned by the General Conference, but also the tradition that the organization has developed, the compromise made when its present structure was designed, and the ideology of both board and staff leaders at any given time.

The result is that several agencies will work in some of the same areas at the same time. For example, when the 1976 General Conference authorized the raising of a substantial sum to combat world hunger, the money was divided among several agencies so that each in its own way could be involved.

When an issue arises that is perceived to be of great importance, the church tends to respond by setting up a new unit of the bureaucracy to deal with it, even though one or more existing agencies are already working on the problem. The civil rights movement of the 1960s produced the Commission on Religion and Race despite the fact that the Board of Church and Society (and its predecessors) had long been giving attention to racial matters. The women's movement resulted in the Commission on the Status and Role of Women even though the Women's Division of the Board of Global Ministries had for many years been a leader in matters relating to women in both the church and society.

The way the several agencies tend to focus on what are perceived to be the most significant issues simply illustrates that there are relatively few causes that capture the attention of the media. Most of the work of the church, like much of life, is routine. The special causes provide color and excitement. Furthermore, having more than one agency working on the same problem is not necessarily bad. Having several organizations giving attention to an issue increases the likelihood that some positive results will be produced.

FUNCTIONS

Distinct from the way the general boards and agencies are formally structured are the five basic functions they all perform. First, they provide a range of services that are useful to the local churches and the clergy. The Methodist Episcopal Church early in the nineteenth century founded a publishing house. The circuit riders needed Bibles, religious books, and tracts, so an organization was created to provide them. Today services provided by general agencies have been expanded beyond printed materials to include films, tapes, fund-raising assistance, loans for building churches, architectural counsel, and leadership training for most officials in the local church.

Second, general agencies carry on ministries on behalf of local churches that require special expertise. The best example is foreign missions. If a denomination is going to send missionaries overseas, it must have an organization to recruit, train, and sustain them. The constituents believe in and support such ministries.

Third, agencies have been created to deal with social issues and to lead the constituents in ways they might not necessarily go if left alone. The task of such agencies is to motivate the church members to change certain attitudes and behavior. Two examples are (1) the Board of Church and Society and (2) the Commission on the Status and Role of Women. The Commission on Religion and Race meets some of the same goals, but it also provides funds to a wide range of ministry projects and causes.

Fourth, certain agencies have a denomination-wide administrative and coordinative function. They collect and distribute funds, make arrangements for the General Conference, and adjudicate disputes between the agencies. The General Council on Ministries and the General Council on Finance and Administration perform these functions.

Fifth, the general agencies figure significantly in the reward or patronage system of the denomination. Election to the board of managers is a recognition of one's valued service in an annual conference. A staff position, particularly at the executive level, has very high status. The general agencies are places to which persons can be promoted. The efforts of women and minorities to ensure that members of their groups secure positions on the boards and staffs illustrate the prestige attached to these posts.

FUNDING

The funding of general church agencies is complex. Since 1924 the principal source of income for the general boards and agencies has been the World Service Fund. The General Conference sets the amount that the churches are asked to raise and the proportion of this amount that each agency will receive. While World Service remains the basic fund, its proportion of the total askings has been decreasing as more special-purpose funds have been authorized.

The special-purpose funds established by the General Conference provide for a variety of needs including black colleges, ministerial education, ethnic congregations, salary and pension subsidies for black pastors, general administration, and support of the bishops. These funds are administered by one or more of the general agencies.

A major source of funds for mission projects is the Advance Special program through which contributions are solicited for specific, authorized projects. Another significant source for mission projects is the collections solicited by local United Methodist Women's groups and channeled through the Women's Division of the Board of Global Ministries. Other funds include bequests, income from endowments, designated gifts, fees for services, and the sale of literature.

RELATIONSHIPS

To understand the general agencies properly, one must understand the nature of their relationship with other parts of the denomination, including the local churches, the annual conferences, the other agencies and the bishops.

The United Methodist Church provides for organizations at all levels that are parallel to most general agencies. For example, there is a General Board of Church and Society based in Washington, D.C. Each annual conference must also have a Board of Church and Society, and every local church a Work Area on Church and Society. These serve as the regional and local outlets for the general agency and provide the leaders to carry out its program. Every general agency needs this system of parallel organizations if it is going to get its message to people at the grass roots and receive financial support from them. Sometimes the terminology becomes a bit incongruous: "The Board of Global Ministries in the Memphis Annual Conference."

The relationship of general agencies with each other can be characterized by one word: competitive. They are competing for the attention, time, and support of United Methodist people so it is only natural that they would be a bit wary of each other. The denomination has long had an organization to coordinate the work of and adjudicate disputes between the agencies. This is a necessary, but not a popular, task and one that never quite satisfies anyone. One reason why the general boards and agencies are not more influential in determining the course of the denomination is that they tend to neutralize each other.

The relationship of the church bureaucracies and the bishops has been in transition. The agencies need the bishops, because their goodwill and favor is critical if financial support is to be forthcoming; yet the agencies correctly perceive the bishops as a threat to their power. Nevertheless, the influence of the bishops on the agencies has been decreasing; fewer bishops now serve on the boards than was previously the case. The nature of the United Methodist structure will ensure some degree of continued tension between the bishops and the general agencies although this will rarely come into public view.

TRENDS OF CHANGE

The general boards and agencies are not static organizations, but undergo continual change, albeit at different rates. Some of the changes that are occurring now can be expected to continue and reveal perceptible trends.

Ministry vs. Service

The first trend has been a shift of the agencies toward involvement in ministry, particularly in areas of social change, and away from a service orientation. An increasing amount of the bureaucracy's time and effort is going into activities that either have had their origin within the agency or deal with broad issues in the society. In both cases, such activities may be a concern of only a small proportion of the United Methodist people and actually be opposed by some of them. The result has been a waning sense of identification of the bureaucrats with their constituency and vice versa. Thus an adversarial relationship exists between some general boards and a significant number of their constituents.

Patronage

Second, the general boards and agencies as a source of patronage has been openly accepted in the past decade or so. The quota system is the best illustration of this trend. Reserving a certain proportion of the positions on the boards of managers and the staff for specific categories of persons makes it clear that individuals are selected on the grounds that people of their sex or race have been excluded in the past. This is a shift from the idea that the individual worked in a church agency to serve the larger good to having the church organization serve certain categories of persons by providing them with what are perceived to be positions of high status. This can have a long-term impact on the role the agencies fulfill if they are perceived to be primarily the preserve of special-interest and ethnic groups and not identified with the broad range of United Methodist people.

Economic Strain

A third factor lies in the economic trends in the larger society. The inflationary spiral during the past two decades has put severe pressure on many institutions, including the churches. While giving to general church causes has increased, it has not kept pace with inflation. In a time of economic stringency, the organization most distant from the source of funds is in the most precarious position. The congregation must meet local expenses first; denominational causes, no matter how worthy, are secondary. If a local church is forced to reduce its budget, the causes most remote will be in greatest jeopardy.

In the past two decades the church has given its general boards and agencies increasingly difficult tasks. It has mandated that the agencies be showcase examples of the denomination's commitment to inclusiveness. The church has made it clear to the agencies that the composition of the board of managers and the professional staff is the top priority. At the same time, it has compelled the agencies to deal with the most complex problems, not only in the church, but in American society and the world: peace and justice, evangelism, ministering to diverse groups, racism, and world hunger. Money is appropriated and the task given to one or more agency. The church appears to feel that it has then fulfilled its responsibility. Whether or not the agencies make any impact at all on the problems assigned to them is never known. One surmises that the church does not really want to know, because there is never any effective evaluation of the various quadrennial programs.

The years since 1972 have seen more reorganization of the general boards and agencies than in any other comparable period. They have been the subject of continual debate and controversy. However, they reflect the denomination that created and sustains them. A church gets the kind of general boards and agencies it really wants and is willing to support.

NOTES

1. *The Book of Discipline of The United Methodist Church, 1984* (Nashville: United Methodist Publishing House, 1984), para. 805.b.
2. Ibid., para. 803.

PART III

UNITED METHODISM IN ITS THIRD CENTURY

Chapter 12

Identity, Diversity, and Authority

Every church has an identity that is its understanding of what God has called it to be and to do. But there is never complete agreement among the members or groups within the church as to exactly what this is. Diversity exists to some degree in all denominations. Such diversity must not only be recognized but dealt with in such a way that there can be unity of purpose. To handle diversity there must be a recognized and accepted authority which can determine what is acceptable belief and practice.

Identity, diversity, and authority are perennial issues for the church, but particularly so for United Methodism. As it moves into its third century, the church is struggling to come to some consensus on these matters. This chapter will examine the three factors in the light of the church's theology and polity.

IDENTITY

Every denomination has an identity that is defined as the way its adherents perceive their church and the way it is perceived by outsiders. A denomination forms its self-understanding by what its members believe, how they organize themselves to carry out their mission, and the way they live individually and collectively. Identity, therefore, is the result of the interaction of theology, polity, and practice.

A denomination's identity is not static; it may change over time. Most changes are the result of many small and perhaps seemingly trivial modifications that in time can add up to a significantly different identity. The present is always built on the past so that what has taken place in the denomination's history continually influences the contemporary church.

Change is almost always the subject of controversy. There will be persons who passionately want the church to move quickly into new and uncharted areas; others, with equal fervor, want things to remain as they are. And there will be some persons who want the church to return to a real or imagined past era. Each has a different concept of what the church ought to be and do, a different sense of their collective identity as United Methodist people.

The identity of The United Methodist Church has been formed by a combination of factors. Some of these have been present from the beginning of the Methodist movement; others were introduced later. The denomination's identity has changed as some factors have been deemphasized while new ones have been given prominence.

In Theology

What a denomination believes about its nature and mission is a major source of its identity. Identity is shaped by the church's theology. The Methodist movement began as a revival. John Wesley's goal was to reform the Church of England; early Methodism was a renewal movement within that church. The emphasis was on repentance, being saved from sin, and fleeing from the wrath to come. Salvation was for all who desired to receive it. The Methodists believed that "whosoever will may come." But Wesley and his early followers were not content with saving souls; the new Christians were expected to live a disciplined life, to witness, and to serve. This emphasis was carried across the Atlantic. Thomas Coke and Francis Asbury, writing to the members of the Methodist Societies in the United States, said:

> We humbly believe that God's design in raising up the preachers called Methodists, in America, was to reform the continent, and spread scriptural holiness over these lands.[1]

The early Methodists placed great stress on Christian perfection and the disciplined life. The converted were to continue to grow in grace. Social structures were provided to ensure that the converts were both assisted and monitored as they struggled to make progress in their spiritual journey. The classes and the bands were the means by which the people received support and encouragement. They were also useful devices in keeping persons from deviating from the straight and narrow way.

From the earliest days, Methodist people sought to improve the lot of the poor and the oppressed. This goes back as early as Wesley's student days and participation in the Holy Club. It continued as the movement developed. The 1784 *Discipline of the Methodist Episcopal Church* stated that the members of the societies should continue to evidence their desire for salvation by doing good of every possible sort to all men. This included doing good to their bodies "by giving food to the hungry, by giving clothing to the naked, by visiting or helping them that are sick or in prison." Also included was doing good "To their souls, by instructing, reproving, or exhorting."[2]

Methodists accepted responsibility for assisting the poor and the oppressed as an expression of their faith that proceeded from their conversion. The combination of an evangelical passion and a concern for the poor has traditionally led to both evangelistic efforts among the lower socioeconomic classes and social reform activities to benefit them. It has involved the church in every major social issue from the anti-slavery movement, to the campaign for Prohibition, to efforts to improve conditions for industrial workers, to the recent civil rights struggles.

The belief that Christians should do something about the evils in the world has made Methodists an active people. They still feel they should do something about problems in the society. This may take various forms, ranging from church people working in local projects, to forming and funding a national church agency to act on their behalf, to attempting to get a governmental agency to take a specific action.

In Polity

Polity, as the way a church organizes itself to carry out its mission, is a visible expression of its theological understandings. The early classes and bands were an example of the way Methodism developed a structure to enforce its understanding of the disciplined life. Because the organization is visible, it is a major source of the denomination's identity.

The fact that Methodism began as an evangelical reform movement led by unusually strong leaders had a great impact on its polity. John Wesley in England and Francis Asbury in America were dominant forces during the formative period. The American church was organized to be episcopal, and the bishops have remained a major force to the present. Methodism has been a church in which the clergy have been dominant. Laity today have a much greater role in both policy making and administration of the denomination, but clergy still tend to hold sway. Moreover, most decisions are made by official but relatively small groups of persons.

The church is not a democratic institution; it never has followed and does not follow the practice of "one person, one vote." Rather, the decision-making groups from the local charge conference to the worldwide General Conference are delegated bodies. Persons are selected as delegates by small official bodies and not by a broad electorate. The delegates to the various conferences may be sensitive to the feelings of the folks back home, but they cannot be instructed how to vote on a particular issue. The principle of delegated conferences has been a part of Methodism since 1808, with the delegates being in the final analysis responsible only to God.

The Methodist denomination has been organized from the top down. The bylaws for the local congregation are designed by a national body. The clergy are sent to local churches, not called by them. The system can be highly efficient, but it requires a high degree of consensus and trust. Both clergy and laity need to have general agreement on the nature and purpose of the church. While groups within the denomination will disagree, there must be areas of broad general agreement on critical areas. The areas of agreement must be perceived as of greater importance than the areas of disagreement. Diversity can be accepted only if there is consensus on those aspects which are perceived to be of greater importance than the differences. If the differences become of greatest importance, schism becomes a possibility.

A high degree of mutual trust is needed at all levels in a denomination that places decision making into the hands of small groups of people. The clergy must trust the bishop that their appointments are fair and in the best interests of the church. Members of a congregation must trust clergy to admit into the ministry only those who have the "gifts and graces." Everyone must trust the members of the charge, annual, jurisdictional, and general conferences to make decisions which are consistent with the beliefs of United Methodists and which will contribute to the church's mission.

The connectional system is at the heart of the denomination's self-understanding. It rests, first, on a consensus of what the church is and what it should do and, second, on mutual trust that all are endeavoring to follow Christ and are working to advance the cause of his church. Only when this consensus exists can a denomination develop the sense of identity that produces the degree of unity necessary for effective witness and ministry.

DIVERSITY

Methodism in the twentieth century has been characterized by theological and social diversity. Diversity, however, always presents a problem for religious groups. Because religion deals with ultimate values, differing viewpoints challenge accepted beliefs. Either the belief that deviates from the norm contains some degree of error, or the official stance is itself not completely correct. Both situations produce some discomfort for people who take their faith seriously. Furthermore, the greater the diversity, the less clear the denomination's sense of identity; it becomes more difficult for the people to know who they are and why they are expected to act in specific ways.

Pluralism in Theology Affirmed

The United Methodist Church in 1972 affirmed pluralism as a principle. *The Discipline* that year stated:

> We do not possess infallible rules to follow, or reflex habits that suffice, or precedents for simple imitation. Whatever may be our differences of heritage or mindset, we are forced to re-examine our convictions and alter our attitudes. . . . In this task of reappraising and applying the Gospel, theological pluralism should be recognized as a principle.[3]

The Discipline goes on to state that theological pluralism must not be confused with "theological indifferentism." Pluralism does not mean that it doesn't matter what you believe as long as you are sincere. Instead, it is an invitation for Christian people to consider their heritage, to discuss their different beliefs, and to relate their faith to the contemporary scene. It is a recognition that there will be differences, but that these can be the starting point toward making the faith relevant for today.

Along with theological pluralism, social diversity is also affirmed. The Social Principles[4] urge the church to minister to the larger society and to provide for the needs of a wide range of groups of persons including families, the divorced, racial and ethnic minorities, religious minorities, children, youth, young adults, the aged, women, and persons with handicapping conditions. To affirm members of these groups, *The Discipline* requires that denominational officials include women, ethnic minorities, youth and persons with handicapping conditions. A degree of social diversity is thus assured.

For church leaders and theologians, pluralism can be a useful principle. The danger is that less thoughtful persons may interpret it to mean "anything, or almost anything, goes." Pluralism as it is presently affirmed encompasses an invitation for all to engage in theological reflection. Unfortunately, pluralism can be used to rationalize a wide range of beliefs and actions, including some that represent drastic departures from traditional United Methodist faith and practice.

It is increasingly evident that pluralism really means a range of acceptable beliefs and practices that must, in fact, have limits. There are some things that a United Methodist cannot believe or do and still remain a member in good standing. The range may be broad, but there are limits. The problem the church now faces is how to define the limits of acceptable belief and action. There is a core of beliefs that has traditionally been part of the Methodist heritage. However, the contemporary church has serious difficulties accepting what might be interpreted as inflexible rules. The affirmation of pluralism as a principle makes it difficult to define what is appropriate belief and practice.

Pluralism in Polity Rejected

Pluralism may be an accepted principle for theology, but not for polity. United Methodists may understand the faith differently, but any deviation from the prescribed form of organization is not tolerated. The quadrennially produced *Discipline* contains bylaws for all parts of the church's organization. Every congregation is expected to be organized in the manner stated. Qualifications for church membership and admission into the ministry are spelled out with the expectation they will be followed throughout the connection.

Unless alternative structures are authorized, both congregations and individuals are expected to follow the procedures spelled out in *The Discipline*. Persons or groups do deviate from the prescribed form occasionally, but this tends to be done quietly and overlooked by denominational officials—either because they do not have the power to impose sanctions, or because the approved organization cannot appropriately deal with the particular instance.

For United Methodists, the test of orthodoxy is not adherence to a creed but conformity to polity procedures prescribed in *The Book of Discipline*. The pastor whose theological beliefs may never be questioned will come under criticism if his church deviates from accepted polity. A denominational official said of an independent-minded minister who had built a large, active congregation, "That congregation is not really a Methodist church; he has a big Baptist church." The man's success was admired and perhaps envied, but he came under criticism for not following the rules precisely.

The most serious controversies within Methodism develop when differences in theology result in clear differences in polity. The battle will be fought, not over the theological issues, but over the form of organization. The arguments tend not to be based on theology, but on such matters as efficiency, economy, and fairness to various persons or groups within the denomination. The underlying issues are theological, but the debates are over the form of organization by which the theology is to be implemented. The matter is eventually resolved by the denomination's approving a specific polity matter that puts the theological assumption into practice.

AUTHORITY

United Methodists have a particularly difficult time with authority for theological issues. The quadrilateral that has been in *The Discipline* since 1972 is a helpful device in setting the criteria for discussion. It cannot resolve specific issues, as people do interpret the Scriptures and the tradition differently. Individual experiences will vary, and even reasonable people arrive at different conclusions.

From time to time the General Conference has set up special commissions to prepare statements on aspects of the faith, the mission of the church, and the ministry. While the work of such groups may be adopted by the General Conference and become the "official" position of the denomination, for all practical purposes they cannot be enforced. Although *The Discipline* states that Methodists are liable to accusation and trial for "disseminating of doctrines contrary to the established standards of doctrine of The United Methodist Church,"[5] the likelihood of this occurring is virtually nonexistent. Heresy trials are not part of the ongoing Methodist tradition. Without an official creed, providing the the clear proof of heresy would be exceedingly difficult.

If the United Methodist Church does not have a clear authority for theological issues, it does for matters of polity. The General Conference is plainly the body that sets the form of the organization for all parts of the church, from the local congregation to the annual conference to the agencies. The General Conference is the only group authorized to speak officially for the denomination. Although many groups within the denomination do speak on a variety of topics, they represent only themselves, not the entire church.

There is a tacit recognition of the fact that the church cannot enforce conformity on matters of belief. Therefore various statements of the General Conference as to the official position of the church do not have the force of law, but instead serve as a principle that it is hoped church members will accept and follow. The General Conference also passes various resolutions that are published in a separate volume.[6] These state the official United Methodist position on scores of religious, social, political, and economic issues.

While theological and other statements are taken with varying degrees of seriousness, organizational matters approved by the General Conference will be implemented. The authority on polity matters is clear and accepted. Therefore a theological principle that can be expressed by a change in the organization will become a part of the denomination. For example, the proposed permanent diaconate would create two categories of ordained clergy (one itinerating and one nonitinerating); it would change Methodism's theological understanding of the ministry.

United Methodists need to realize that theology and polity are intertwined; they cannot be separated. When the General Conference or some other body tinkers with the ecclesiastical machinery, it is usually doing much more than simply changing the organizational form. It may be altering the theological assumptions of which the organization is an expression. Thus a change in the duties of the bishop has implications for the theology of the episcopacy. Altering the clergy orders has an impact on the theology of ordination. And a debate over who is authorized to administer Communion is a debate over the nature of the sacraments.

This is not to say that theology and polity should not be discussed and changes sometimes made. It is important that the relationship between theology and polity be clearly understood so that changes can be made intelligently and that these can be consistent with the tradition and mission of the United Methodist Church.

NOTES

1. *The Methodist Discipline of 1798,* facsimile edition edited by Frederick A. Norwood (Rutland, Vt.: Academy Books, 1979), p. iii.
2. Ibid., p. 133.
3. *The Book of Discipline of The United Methodist Church, 1971* (Nashville: United Methodist Publishing House, 1972), para. 70, p. 69.
4. *The Book of Discipline of The United Methodist Church, 1984* (Nashville: United Methodist Publishing House, 1984), para. 70, pp. 86–104.
5. Ibid., para. 2621.1.
6. *The Book of Resolutions of The United Methodist Church* (Nashville: United Methodist Publishing House, 1984).

Chapter 13

The Idea of Itineracy

From its beginning, the itinerant minister has been a vital and unique aspect of Methodism. Ministers have moved at fairly frequent intervals. In the early days of the denomination the circuit riders were reassigned every several months. Today every United Methodist minister is appointed to a church or other appropriate place of service annually. While most will be reappointed to the same place for several years, the expectation by both the clergy and the laity is that the minister will move to a different charge usually every four to six years.

The itinerant system is the result of the interaction of certain theological assumptions, historical events and denominational structures. Today the itineracy is under great pressure. This is already having an impact on the system that may result in fundamental changes.

COMPONENTS OF ITINERACY

The first component of an itinerant system is the perception of the church as having a clearly understood mission in the world. The theology underlying the itineracy is missional. The mission of the church takes priority over the desires of both the clergy and the congregation. The pastor is willing to go where needed to enable the church to achieve its goals. Personal considerations are secondary. It was this understanding of their task that led the early circuit riders to accept appointments to the wilderness that was the American frontier. The church's goal to reform the continent and spread scriptural holiness was of the utmost importance, and individual desires were not permitted to interfere.

The second component of the itineracy is the willingness to trust the judgment of the church as to where an individual can be of greatest service. Methodist pastors are in a real sense persons under orders. They place their lives in the hands of the bishop, who, with the advice of the district superintendents, determines where they will work and where they will live.

Likewise, a congregation accepts the judgment of the cabinet regarding which minister is most appropriate for its church at a given time. The congregation must be willing to receive and support whomever the bishop appoints. This requires a high level of trust by both the clergy and the laity. For the itinerant system to function, both parties must have confidence that the bishop will act to further the mission of the church by providing the best pastor available to a congregation. They must believe that whatever sacrifices or inconveniences either must accept are for the purpose of attaining a larger and more important goal.

The third component of the itineracy is the assumption that a frequent change of ministers is desirable for both the minister and the congregation. While individuals may have different gifts and graces, it is assumed that ministers are to some degree interchangeable. Thus frequent ministerial moves will allow a greater number of congregations to benefit from the talents (or suffer through the shortcomings) of a greater number of pastors.

Furthermore, it is assumed that frequent changes of pastors will bring a variety of approaches to ministry to a particular church. This can bring a freshness to the church program that is considered beneficial to all. The church gets a different leadership style; the minister is forced to adapt to a new set of circumstances. Both may be enriched and grow in the process.

The fourth component of the itinerant system has been a relatively homogenous group of traveling elders. Many ministerial members of annual conferences are white males who can move on short notice. They and their families accept mobility as a way of life. A bishop at any given time has a limited number of pastoral charges to which someone can be appointed. With a more or less homogeneous group of clergy, it is usually possible to find two or three churches which are suited to a particular minister's skills and experience and which would be willing to receive the person as pastor.

A fifth component is the availability of housing. The early circuit riders literally had no home of their own but were given shelter by families as they passed through. Within three decades of the founding of the church in America, consideration was being given to having the congregation provide a dwelling for the minister. As the nation grew and became more urbanized, the church-owned parsonage became a standard feature in Methodism.

The parsonage system is necessary if ministers are to move often. If housing were not provided, the minister could not move on short notice and immediately begin work in a new church. Securing and disposing of houses as a private citizen is arduous, time-consuming, and generally expensive. Furthermore, many United Methodist churches are in rural communities and small towns where housing options are extremely limited. Even in urban areas it may be difficult for a minister to secure a place to live in the community served by that congregation. The church-owned parsonage is essential to the United Methodist system of an itinerant clergy.

IMPACT ON CONFERENCE MEMBERS

The itineracy system has had an important impact on the way Methodist ministers relate to annual conferences. They have their primary ties with an annual conference rather than a particular congregation. The minister's membership is not in the local church that he or she serves, but in the annual conference. It is the ministerial members of an annual conference who admit them into the ministry. They are ordained by the bishop at a session of an annual conference. Their appointments are made at a session of an annual conference. Certain conditions of their employment are determined by their annual conference, including the minimum salary, fringe benefits such as life and medical insurance, travel expenses, continuing education requirements, and whether the parsonage is or is not furnished. When ministers wish to retire, it is the annual conference which votes that relationship and determines the pension program that will define their retirement income.

Because the United Methodist minister moves frequently, the annual conference has tended to be both a fellowship group and a professional society. Ministers have identified with and have had a high degree of allegiance to the annual conference in which they hold membership. While they may serve a number of congregations during their lifetime, the annual conference is where they have their "church" membership.

For the United Methodist minister, the itinerant system has been a combination of rights and obligations. As a member in full connection, the individual has a right to an appointment somewhere in the annual conference with a salary at least equal to the minimum. Ministers do not have a right to be assigned to any particular type of church or to one in a specific geographical area; they are guaranteed only an appointment somewhere in the conference.

The obligation of the minister is to be willing to accept the appointment. While the bishop may attempt to accommodate the needs and wishes of a pastor, the bottom line is that a minister must accept the appointment if he or she wishes to remain a full member of the annual conference.

PRESSURES ON THE ITINERACY

While the itineracy has survived through the entire history of American Methodism, certain factors are bringing pressures on that system. Some of these are trends in the larger society that are having an impact on the church. Others are events and attitudes within the church itself.

The itineracy system has understandably been the subject of debate throughout the life of the church. It was a cause of the first schism in 1792, when James O'Kelly and his followers withdrew when they were unsuccessful in getting a proposal adopted that would have allowed the annual conference to overturn a bishop's appointment on appeal from a minister. The bishops still assign the clergy, but in a much less arbitrary manner and subject to more restraints than earlier, as explained in chapter 10.

One source of pressure on the itineracy is the increasing expectation within the society for institutions to adapt to the needs of the individual. Related to this is the expectation that persons will have a greater say about those things that have an impact on their lives—for example, where they reside and conditions of their employment. The concept of increased participation by individuals in decisions affecting them has permeated much of American life, including the church.

A visible result of this in the United Methodist Church is the consultation regarding appointments that must take place between the bishop (or the district superintendent), the pastor, and the pastor-parish relations committee. The process requires the district superintendent to "identify the pastor's gifts, graces and professional experience and expectations, and also the needs and concerns of the pastor's spouse and family."[1] Various aspects of the congregation such as size, theological stance, needs, and community setting are to be considered when appointments are being made. Although *The Discipline* states that consultation is not the same as calling a pastor, the fact is that this process, if strictly followed, has the effect of limiting the power of the bishops to assign pastors where they think they can be of greatest service to the church. As more persons have a say in the appointment of pastors, the pressure to modify the itinerant system will increase.

A second factor putting pressure on the itineracy is an increasingly heterogeneous clergy. Annual conferences whose ministerial members only two decades ago consisted largely of either white or black males have become much more heterogeneous. First, the white and black conferences merged. Second, the number of women clergy and clergy couples has increased dramatically. Third, the number of non-English-speaking churches has also grown. The result is a more complex set of factors to take into account in assigning ministers. Some churches will resist the appointment of a pastor of another race; others do not wish to have a woman pastor. The congregation that has a Spanish or Korean constituency needs a minister who is fluent in the appropriate language.

A third source of pressure is the increased number of employed spouses. This is causing a growing proportion of clergy to want to remain in the same locale for long periods of time. A minister's moving can result in a drastic reduction in family income if the spouse is forced to give up his or her position. The growing number of women clergy will make this matter more acute. While there is still a fairly large number of ministers' wives who are not employed outside the home, there are few ministers' husbands who are not employed. Thus a move for a married woman pastor almost always affects the spouse's employment.

The resistance to relocating is already causing noticeable tension in some annual conferences. The pastor who would like to serve in a particular city for a term is denied the opportunity; the person already there resists moving because of a spouse's career. The opportunities available to those who are willing to relocate are therefore restricted.

AFFIRMATION OR ALTERNATIVES

As Methodism enters its third century, it is unclear just what direction the itinerant system will take. The pressures for change are strong, and some major alterations such as the consultation process have already been enacted by the General Conference. The desire by both clergy and laity to have more say in the appointment process will probably continue. The growing number of two-career couples will make relocation difficult for many ministerial families.

One possible course would be for the church to insist that the minister is an itinerant and is expected to go where sent. This would mean more persons leaving the ministry, which is what happened in the early days of the church as individuals left the traveling ministry to locate or settle in one place. The 1984 General Conference, in an attempt to strengthen the itineracy, added to the responsibilities of the Administrative Board,

> to provide adequate housing for the pastor(s). Housing shall not be considered as part of compensation or remuneration, but shall be considered as a means provided by the local church, and for the convenience of the local church, to enable its ministry and the itinerant ministry of the Annual Conference.[2]

By contrast, the 1976 *Discipline* simply instructed the Pastor-Parish Relations Committee to consult on such matters as "salary, travel expenses, vacation, health and life insurance, pension, continuing education, housing and other practical matters . . . and make recommendations to the Administrative Board."[3] In 1980 the Administrative Board was instructed to review the recommendation of the Pastor-Parish Relations Committee regarding housing for the minister. *The Discipline* stated, "It is the responsibility of the Administrative Board to provide adequate housing for the pastor."[4] Instructing the church to provide housing is a way of strengthening the itineracy.

Another possibility would be to develop some type of modified call system in which both the pastor and the congregation will have greater freedom to negotiate. A pastor could seek the locale where he or she wanted to live. The clergy would have to trade the security of the guaranteed appointment for the freedom of having a greater voice in determining which church and which community they will serve.

If the clergy had the freedom to decide where they would and would not serve, the congregation would also determine whom they could accept. More time would be necessary to secure a minister, because the selection process takes time. Terminating a minister's relationship with a congregation would become awkward if he or she could not simply be appointed elsewhere by the bishop. More important, such a change would fundamentally alter Methodism's theology of a "sent" rather than "called" ministry.

The proposal to the 1984 General Conference to establish the office of a nonitinerating, ordained, permanent deacon was in reality an attempt to have it both ways. Having two classes of ordained clergy as voting members of the annual conference would provide for ordained itinerating and nonitinerating clergy. The elders would continue to be appointed by the bishop; they would go where sent and retain the guaranteed appointment. The deacons would secure their own positions and then be appointed by the bishop, who would have veto power over a particular assignment.

While the original proposal included among the proposed deacons a range of congregational and church institution staff members, it is not inconceivable that in due time Methodism would develop two categories of ordained clergy competing with each other for positions within both the congregations and ecclesiastical institutional structures. One group would be assigned by the bishop; the other would secure their own positions in local churches and institutions. While the proposal was rejected and the matter referred to a committee for further study, it is probable that the issue will arise again.

The itineracy has served American Methodism well. It is a system that gives the mission of the church a higher priority than the personal needs and desires of the individual. The minister submits to the judgment of the bishop, who determines where his or her talents can best be used. The itineracy is demanding because of what it requires of the clergy. In the early days of the church in America, the mortality and dropout rates among the traveling preachers were high. While clerical life today is not so rigorous, not everyone is able to accept the requirements of the itineracy, which include moving with some degree of regularity, adjusting to different communities and congregations, and placing one's calling ahead of personal and family wishes and needs.

The Methodist itineracy has, of course, changed over the years and will continue to do so as the church moves into its third century. Whatever changes do occur, it is hoped that the method of placing ministers will continue to be based on the missional needs of the church and that clergy will be sent where their gifts and graces can be most effectively employed in witness and ministry.

NOTES

1. *The Book of Discipline of The United Methodist Church, 1984* (Nashville: United Methodist Publishing House, 1984), para. 531.2.
2. Ibid., para. 256.3d.
3. *The Book of Discipline of The United Methodist Church, 1976* (Nashville: United Methodist Publishing House, 1976), para. 260.2d (4).
4. *The Book of Discipline of The United Methodist Church, 1980* (Nashville: United Methodist Publishing House, 1980), para. 255.3f.

Chapter 14

United Methodism as a World Church

While Americans constitute 95 percent of the members of the United Methodist Church, the denomination is nevertheless a world church. Methodism has never perceived itself as a strictly national denomination. In the early days of the church there were formal ties with John Wesley and his movement in England, until the Revolutionary War and the rapid growth of the church in America made the separation of British and American Methodism inevitable.

Methodism has always been a church with a missionary thrust. It has never been content to minister only at home, but has felt a responsibility to preach the gospel throughout the world to those who have not heard it. John Wesley's oft-quoted statement "The world is my parish" has been taken literally. The church in the colonies was to a great degree the result of the work of persons sent by Wesley, particularly

Francis Asbury. In the late eighteenth century Methodism was also carried to the Caribbean by missionaries from Great Britain. Thomas Coke, who had a part in bringing Methodism to America, died while en route to India.

Only thirty-five years after the Methodist Episcopal Church was founded at the Christmas Conference of 1784, the Missionary Society was organized. From a small beginning it grew into an agency that in time commissioned thousands of missionaries who have served the world over. Both American and British Methodism were deeply involved in the missionary movement, establishing Methodist churches in all parts of the world. Some of these continue to be an integral part of United Methodism, while others are autonomous churches but affiliated. Still others have no formal ties, but are part of the World Methodist Council. Contemporary Methodism is global in its scope.

THE CENTRAL CONFERENCE

United Methodists outside the United States are organized into central conferences. These are regional bodies and function much like the American jurisdictions. Each central conference consists of one or more annual conferences or provisional annual conferences.[1] The latter are small mission organizations that do not have the resources to be annual conferences. There are seven central conferences, including four in Europe, two in Africa, and one in the Philippines. Within these central conferences are twenty-nine annual conferences and nine provisional annual conferences. The central conferences elect bishops, who are members of the Council of Bishops. They have freedom to adapt to particular situations in the countries where the churches are located.

Membership in the United Methodist Church outside the United States stood at 453,123 in 1985. The trend in the 1970s was downward, but since 1981 the membership has been growing. There are 4,224 organized churches and 9,307 Sunday schools with an enrollment of 241,086. The central conferences have 2,508 ordained ministers and 1,248 supply pastors. In 1970 there were 563 missionaries in the central conferences; in 1985 this number had decreased to 93. Of these, 71 were in Africa, 12 in Europe, and 10 in the Philippines.

Sixty percent of the central conference members are in Africa. The next largest groups (20 percent) are in the Philippines and in Europe. Although the numbers may be relatively small, United Methodism has a presence in such places as Hungary, where there are ten churches; Estonia (USSR), fifteen churches; and Poland, forty-six churches.

Over the past decade the total membership of the United Methodist Church outside the United States has fluctuated between 400,000 and 500,000. It is hazardous to generalize about trends because of the difficulty of securing accurate statistics from such widely scattered groups.

The people who are members of central conference churches are an integral part of United Methodism. While they are authorized to make adjustments in local structures appropriate to the social and political conditions in their locality, they participate in all parts of the connectional system. A European bishop served as a president of the Council of Bishops for the first time in the year 1985–86. Delegates from outside the United States participate in the General Conference. At the 1984 session, arrangements were made for simultaneous translation of the proceedings into several languages, making it possible for persons without a command of English to participate.

In the period ahead, United Methodism will become increasingly aware of its identity as a world church. The ease of communications and the jet plane have made it possible for the far-flung branches of Methodism to have increased contact with one another. The church will, therefore, find it easier to function as a worldwide organization.

AFFILIATED AUTONOMOUS CHURCHES

Twenty-eight autonomous Methodist denominations throughout the world have a covenant relationship with the

United Methodist Church and are listed as Affiliated Autonomous Churches. Most of these spring from Methodist and Evangelical United Brethren missionary activities over the past century and a half. The rise of political nationalism in the twentieth century has had its counterpart in the church; most autonomous churches consist of Methodists in a particular country such as Brazil, Costa Rica, or Singapore.

The covenant relationship between the United Methodist Church and the Affiliated Autonomous Churches provides for the mutual recognition of members. Ministers may transfer between the denominations with the consent of the bishops or other appointive authority. Affiliated Autonomous Churches are entitled to two delegates, one clergy and one layperson, to the United Methodist General Conference. These delegates are entitled to all the rights and privileges except the right to vote. A plan of mutual visitation may be arranged by the Council of Bishops with their counterparts in the other churches.

In 1985, nineteen of the twenty-six Affiliated Autonomous Churches reported 760,901 full members and 5,915 congregations. There were 5,760 ordained ministers and 1,544 approved supply pastors, and a total of 366 missionaries were serving in these churches.

While the accuracy of the statistics cannot be verified, the overall trends are encouraging. During the period 1970–1985 the number of members and congregations grew significantly. The number of both ordained and approved supply pastors has also been increasing, allowing by contrast a decrease since 1970 of almost one-third the number of missionaries serving these churches.

The relationship of the Affiliated Autonomous Churches with the United Methodist Church is one of great flexibility. It enables the denominations to maintain contact and to work together. It enables American Methodism to assist where desired with personnel and financial support. In turn, the Affiliated Autonomous Churches contribute through their representation in United Methodist bodies and their participation in other connectional activities.

WORLD METHODIST COUNCIL

A visible sign of the global dimensions of the Methodist movement is the World Methodist Council. This is an association of twenty-one different Methodist bodies located in eighty-six countries. The constitution states as its purpose, "it does not seek to legislate for them nor to invade their autonomy." Rather, it exists "to serve them and to give unity to their witness and enterprise."[2]

Although the World Methodist Council has existed only since 1951, it succeeded a series of Ecumenical Methodist Conferences that began in 1881. These included representatives of the American branches of Methodism and churches around the world. The conferences were held every ten years, except for 1941, which was during World War II.

The headquarters of the World Methodist Council is in Lake Junaluska, North Carolina, including offices, a library, and a collection of Wesleyana. There is also an office in Geneva, Switzerland. The council now meets every five years. The council has sponsored various publications, including *Who's Who in Methodism,* an *Album of Methodist History,* and *The Encyclopedia of World Methodism.*

The meetings of the council provide an opportunity for Methodist leaders from all over the world to become acquainted. It is an occasion for the preparation of papers on Methodist theology that have resulted in published books.

Every four years the council sponsors the Oxford Institute of Methodist Theological Studies, in which one hundred scholars from all branches of Methodism participate. The council also initiated an exchange program between pastors in different countries and has sponsored programs on topics like evangelism and congregational development.

The World Methodist Council serves first as a visible symbol of the worldwide nature of Methodism. It also provides a means by which the followers of John Wesley who now live in widely divergent social systems can share their insights and experiences and be supportive of each other.

STRUCTURE FOR A WORLD CHURCH

The relationship between the United Methodist Church in America and Methodist bodies in other countries represents the denomination's practical approach to expressing its theology through its polity. First, there is the clear understanding of and commitment to the concept that the church is worldwide. It transcends national boundaries as well as those of race, language, and culture. Given this basic assumption, a range of organizational structures has been created to accommodate the different cultural, social, and political contexts in which the churches must operate. The theological concept of unity is maintained by connectional relationship between the various Methodist bodies.

The central conferences, which are an integral part of United Methodism, can make organizational adjustments as appropriate to enable them to operate in their particular situations. The Affiliated Autonomous Churches are independent groups, but continue to have a formal and specified relationship with United Methodism. Leaders from all Methodist bodies are brought together every five years to consider matters of theology and mutual interest. In these ways Methodism finds its expression as a world church and seeks to bridge the cultural and political differences among the peoples and countries of the world.

NOTES

1. *The Discipline* provides that "because of geographical, language, political or other considerations," churches may be organized into provisional central conferences (*Discipline, 1984*, para. 639).

2. Nolan B. Harmon, ed., *The Encyclopedia of World Methodism*, vol. 2 (Nashville: United Methodist Publishing House, 1974), p. 2602.

Chapter 15

United Methodism and the Conciliar Movement

Methodists have participated in the ecumenical movement in its various forms since its beginnings. United Methodism has never conceived of itself as an exclusive group, but rather as one vital part of the universal church. This perception is expressed officially in its Constitution, which states, "As part of the Church Universal, The United Methodist Church believes that the Lord of the Church is calling Christians everywhere to strive toward unity; and therefore it will seek, and work for, unity at all levels of church life."[1]

Despite this supportive role, the ecumenical movement has had little direct impact on the life and work of the average Methodist minister and layperson. This chapter will examine the nature of the movement, its institutional expression, and how United Methodists relate to these.

COMPONENTS OF ECUMENISM

Most clergy and church members in the mainline denominations look favorably on the ecumenical movement. They also give it little thought beyond an occasional affirmation and have little personal involvement beyond participating in a local program such as a cooperative food pantry or a city ministerial association. Most Christians, including United Methodists, live and move and have their being within their own denominations.

The denomination is, in fact, the way churches in America have been organized. From time to time interdenominational agencies have been created to perform functions that can be done better cooperatively. Some of these have a long history, including the American Bible Society (1816), the American Sunday School Union (1824), the Evangelical Alliance (1867), and the Student Volunteer Movement (1886). Some agencies continue; some have become part of other organizations. State and city councils of churches were formed to enable denominations to widen the range of cooperative activities and programs. These had their beginnings around the turn of the century and have continued to the present. Methodists have always participated in these organizations.

It is easy to understand why the cooperative movement began when it did. American society in the late nineteenth century was undergoing sweeping social, economic, and industrial changes. The frontier no longer existed. Vast numbers of immigrants were arriving and settling in the cities, where they provided the work force for expanding industries. Living and working conditions in the great cities aroused the conscience of Christian people. The bitterness and violence of the labor conflicts such as the railroad strike of 1877, the Haymarket riot in Chicago in 1866, the Homestead (Pennsylvania) steel strike of 1892 and the Pullman Company strike of 1894 convinced church leaders that action was needed. The magnitude and complexity of the problems were major factors in the denominations' working together to seek solutions. The councils of churches were one result. The Federal Council of Churches represented the denominations' attempts to deal with social and economic issues on a large scale.

The ecumenical movement was also born at a time that coincided with the development of big business in America. The giant corporation was seen by church leaders as the model to be followed. Businesses were consolidating, and this was viewed as helpful to economic progress. Using big business as the model, consolidation of the denominations became the goal of the ecumenical movement.

Some denominational leaders involved in the ecumenical movement still have the corporation as their model. While the society continues to challenge the dominance of business and industrial giants, certain denominational leaders are still striving to create a religious monopoly. This is based on the assumptions that a monolithic church would be more effective and that the unity of the church is the will of God. For some this is not debatable, as late W. A. Visser 't Hooft made clear in an address in 1957:

> God sees us as one people, one family. . . . in God's sight there is just one body of those who have heard his call and respond to it. God's church cannot be divided because its unity belongs to its very essence.[2]

From this assumption of unity it follows that denominations are human creations which are contrary to the will of God. To argue that the function of the different churches is to meet the needs of different groups of people is dismissed as capitulating to human will rather than accepting God's will.

Unity, however, can be defined in different ways. A source of confusion has been a tendency to vacillate between unity theologically defined and unity sociologically defined. Unity can be a theological concept whereby all those who owe allegiance to Christ have a sense of oneness. This unity can be affirmed despite a broad range of differences in polity, style of worship, social class, race, or culture. However, when unity is made a sociological concept, it requires a single social organization. The Christian church can have unity in a theological sense and still be organized into a variety of denominations; to have sociological unity, the denominations must be combined into a single church. Taking the latter seriously leads the person who believes this to be the will of God either to wait for a miracle or to sink into despair.

Throughout the twentieth century there have been serious proposals to form a united church. The last was the Blake-Pike proposal in 1960, which led to the formation of the Commission on Church Union (COCU) and a proposal for the still nonexistent Church of Christ Uniting. Such proposals and the resulting organization provide a forum for discussion in which Methodists have participated fully. While this has been generally positive, there is no evidence that the process has brought the creation of a united church any nearer. Indeed, given the history of church mergers in the twentieth century, a uniting of several mainline denominations would alter the religious landscape only slightly. It would not reduce the number of denominations, for mergers usually result in the creation of a "new" church whose members want to maintain the tradition that they fear will be lost.

INSTITUTIONAL EXPRESSIONS OF ECUMENICITY

There are two types of ecumenical organizations in which United Methodists participate. The first are special-purpose groups organized to do a specific task that can be accomplished more effectively by churches working together. Many of these are local: a soup kitchen, a shelter for the homeless, a food pantry, or a contact ministry in which phones are manned by volunteers to deal with persons in crisis situations. These require the participation and support of individuals and local congregations. Other special purpose agencies such as the American Bible Society and certain relief agencies are national or even worldwide in scope. Participation is by financial support from the denomination's benevolence budget, with some contributions by individuals.

The second type is the council of churches, which is

multipurpose and engages in a variety of activities. There are councils at various levels: city/metropolitan, state, the National Council of Churches, and the World Council of Churches. It is noteworthy that a denomination, not the church members, has membership in the councils. The participating denominations select persons to be their representatives on the governing board, which is the council. The denominations also provide the funds that enable the council to employ professional staff and carry out its programs.

The United Methodist Church has participated in the various councils since their inception. A fund entitled the Interdenominational Cooperation Fund (ICF) is currently collected from each local church for the support of the National and World Council of Churches. This fund, however, represents only a small proportion of the United Methodist money that goes into these councils. The general boards and agencies channel an amount several times that of the ICF into the councils' various departments and programs. In 1983 the general church boards and agencies channeled seven times more money to the World Council of Churches than did the ICF[3] and twelve times more money to the National Council of Churches.[4] These data illustrate the extent of United Methodism's financial commitment to these conciliar organizations. The more than nine million dollars contributed to these two councils represented 11.9 percent of all the general benevolence and administrative funds of the United Methodist Church.[5]

The official United Methodist link with other denominations and other ecumenical organizations is the General Commission on Christian Unity and Interreligious Concerns. Its mandate is "To advocate and work toward the full reception of Christian unity in every aspect of the churches' life and . . . to advocate and work for the establishment and strengthening of relationship with other living faiths."[6] There are other unofficial links, because virtually every general board is involved with other denominational and ecumenical agencies that are working in similar areas of interest.

The General Commission on Christian Unity and Interreligious Concerns perceives its mandate of working for Christian unity at all levels of church life to include the merger of the various denominations. The commission's report to the 1984 General Conference affirmed, "The conviction that the very dividedness of the Church of Jesus Christ hinders the mission of the church in and for the world instructs every one of our program strategies."[7]

The commission's activities consist of training events or workshops for groups around the church to promote ecumenical concerns including advancing the work of the world and national councils. It has been involved in arranging dialogues between United Methodists and representatives of other denominations on theological issues.

Each local church is expected to have a work area on Christian Unity and Interreligious Concerns. The task of this group is to encourage awareness and understanding of ecumenism at all levels. A similar body is charged with performing this task on the annual conference level.

A UNITED METHODIST PERSPECTIVE

United Methodism, by the nature of its character and history, is in a unique position in relation to other churches. It is a denomination that stands between the Catholic and Reformed traditions. It contains elements of each but is not wholly identified with either.

The Methodist movement emerged from the Church of England, which had separated from the Roman Catholic Church primarily for political, not theological reasons. While changes occurred, the break was not as drastic as in other movements. John Wesley remained a priest in the Church of England to the end of his life. From its Anglican roots, Methodism inherited a catholic tradition. The teachings of the reformers also had an influence on Methodism, particularly in America. The evangelical fervor of the movement, the independent spirit, and the role of the laity in leadership reflect the influence of the free churches.

Methodism began as a reform movement within the

Church of England; its goal was not to establish a new denomination. Established social institutions rarely can adapt rapidly enough to meet the expectations of radical reformers, and the Church of England in the eighteenth century was no exception. So the Methodist movement evolved into a separate church. It was eminently practical as it adapted its organization to achieve its theological goals. This practical characteristic has enabled Methodism to adjust to changing situations and to work with other denominations to achieve mutually desired goals.

The United Methodist Church encompasses a wide range of social and theological diversity as expressed in its wide geographic distribution of local churches. United Methodist congregations can be found in almost every section and virtually every type of community in America. Few denominations have the broad social diversity of the United Methodists, a diversity that is expressed in styles of worship and local church programs.

Within the Wesleyan tradition Methodists have usually encompassed a range of theological diversity. This diversity has been perceived as a positive characteristic. Doctrine is perceived as dynamic.

> Theological reflections do change as Christians become aware of new issues and crises. The Church's role in this tenuous process is to provide a stable and sustaining environment in which theological conflict can be constructive and productive. . . . No single creed or doctrinal summary can adequately serve the needs and intentions of United Methodists in confessing their faith or in celebrating their Christian experience.[8]

The United Methodist Church can be expected to continue to participate in the ecumenical movement in its various forms. That movement itself is in a state of transition. The denominations that have been the mainstay of the cooperative groups are losing preeminence to groups that have not been part of the ecumenical movement. It is unclear what the future of the ecumenical organizations will be.

United Methodism has been a practical denomination

that will continue to participate in and support those ecumenical activities which strengthen the witness of the gospel and the ministry of the church. It has confidence that it has a unique contribution to make to this task. And it realizes that church organizations, even ecumenical ones, are transitory, designed to meet the religious needs of people in a particular period of history.

NOTES

1. *The Book of Discipline of The United Methodist Church, 1984* (Nashville: United Methodist Publishing House, 1984), para. 5.
2. Paul S. Minear, *The Nature of the Unity We Seek* (St. Louis: Bethany Press, 1958), p. 123.
3. *Report of the Conciliar Review Committee to the Council of Bishops* (Nashville: United Methodist Publishing House, April, 1984), p. 17.
4. Ibid., p. 30.
5. *Daily Christian Advocate*, Advance Edition K (1 March 1984): K–7.
6. *Discipline, 1984*, para. 2002.1–2002.2.
7. *Daily Christian Advocate*, Advanced Edition J (1 March 1984): J–33.
8. *Discipline, 1984*, para. 69.

Chapter 16

A Unity of Theology and Polity

In the United Methodist Church, theology and polity cannot be adequately understood separately. While we may not give much thought to the theological assumptions on which our institutional structures and ways of doing things are based, these assumptions determine our actions. How we carry out our mission in the world also helps shape our beliefs. What we believe and how we order our life together as a church determines our identity. For the church to be effective, it is necessary for United Methodist people to be clear not only on what they believe, but how these beliefs determine the way the denomination functions; likewise, our actions and organization must be consistent with our beliefs.

It should be clear from the foregoing discussion that theology is the basis of a vital church. This is not a point of controversy, but it can be easily forgotten in the day-to-day operation of the church. Institutional matters can become the driving force and consuming passion. Persons at all levels of the church are subject to the malady of institutionalism. Theology, however, must be returned to its basic role. This can be fostered by remembering the functions of theology, particularly as they relate to polity.

THE FUNCTIONS OF THEOLOGY

At least six functions of theology in relation to polity can be identified.

First, theology inspires the church's vision. It enables persons to see the challenges, to be motivated by them, and to develop ways of carrying out their mission in the world. The Wesleyan heritage is filled with opportunities to catch the vision of what it means to be God's people. But that heritage must be known if it is to inspire us.

Second, theology helps shape the church's identity. It provides a means of answering the questions, "Who are we, and what should we be and do?" At this point, the more recent commitment to *theological* pluralism must be examined.[1] It was previously stated that pluralism as a recognition of valid differences is inevitable and part of our heritage. But widely varying, inconsistently interpreted, and blatantly open-ended constructions of theology have lessened our ability to achieve a sense of identity. The frustration over a lack of clarity in what we believe can lead to an almost frenzied emphasis on programs of good works. This lack of consensus regarding our identity can result in a diffuse and weakened church.

Third, theology directs polity. The church's fundamental beliefs provide the focus and form of its institutional structures. Without the right theological undergirding, the institution is like a plant with shallow roots. Theology generates mission, and mission determines polity. Polity provides a way for testing the validity of theology. However, when much time, legislation, finances, and energy are devoted to maintaining our structures, it is possible to wonder if we have not reached a point where the institution has become an end in itself. The church fails in its mission if it becomes only a social institution, albeit one that serves useful functions.

Fourth, theology provides a basis for accountability. An understanding of theology and doctrine enables us to know when we are minimizing, ignoring, or departing from what we believe we are supposed to be and do. Fuzzy and vague statements of faith leave us without an adequate means of judging accountability. Accountability is not the imposition of an inquisitional spirit; it is the use of theology to create a directional spirit, much like a compass. We need to know where the theological north is and be able to intelligently assess degrees of variance from our controlling convictions.

Fifth, theology evokes evaluation. It serves as a necessary filter through which to pour the mass of proposed legislation and institutional structures. It can help to keep unhealthy contaminants and impurities from passing through. It can help the church move toward higher levels of righteousness, effective ministry, and efficiency. Theology enables the church to continually examine itself to see whether it is achieving its goals.

Sixth, theology is the basis for renewal. Because the church in the world never fully lives up to its theological expectations, renewal is always in order somewhere in the institution. But such renewal can only be accomplished by people who are bonded to their beliefs rather than only to the institution. When polity dominates, maintaining the institution becomes the controlling factor. Some persons will be threatened; any attempt at renewal will be resisted. As used here, "renewal" does not mean that everything is continually up for grabs. Rather, it means that committed, intelligent, and discerning people will be motivated by their theology to work on specific areas of weakness so that the church may become more fully the body of Christ.

These are some of the more important functions of theology in relation to polity. The church is sometimes criticized for being too theological. And if by this critics mean the church is detached and made up of irrelevant people who live in ivory towers, the critique should be heeded. However, the opposite may be true; the church may not have been theological enough. The light that our Wesleyan heritage can shed on the life of the church may have been obscured. The church may be floundering in part because of theological amnesia. With such forgetfulness, the church may be guided by other principles and standards. The result is an institution that looks and acts more like a corporation than a community of faith. And ironically, polity becomes more legalistic than sound theology would ever allow.

THE FUNCTION OF POLITY

Polity provides the institutional structures by which the church carries out its mission in the world. Witnessing to the gospel and ministering are complex tasks. A multitude of decisions must be made and ways developed so that things can be done decently and in order. Leaders must be selected in ways that will be accepted as legitimate. A process by which the call of those wishing to enter the ordained ministry is appropriately tested and its validity affirmed or denied must be implemented. Membership standards must be determined; program emphases decided upon and implemented. Budgets must be prepared, raised, and expended. Property must be bought, sold, and maintained. There is an ever-present danger that the institution will become an end in itself instead of a means to a greater end.

There is also an immediacy about institutional matters that requires specific decisions by a certain date. One bishop commented about an inner city church, "Should we attempt to keep the church open? If so, what type of pastor should I appoint? These decisions must be made by the end of the month." The bishop knew that failure to act meant a decision by default. Institutional pressures can be intense; they cannot be avoided.

Both the process by which decisions are made and the decisions themselves should be consistent with the understanding of the nature and mission of the church. Here again, the leaders face a difficult task because the issues are rarely clear-cut. Decisions become difficult when not all the facts are available and when the consequences are uncertain; but judgments must be made nevertheless.

For United Methodists, polity is more than the institutional expression of theological assumptions. Polity is continually in the process of forming theology. Faith and practice are inseparable; they are opposite sides of the same coin. The church does not begin with a theology which it then applies; it engages in mission, and this experience helps shape its theology.

Polity provides the method of testing the validity of our theological assumptions. Beliefs must in fact work in the world where Christians live and move and have their being. Religious groups from time to time have attempted to adhere to beliefs that simply could not be put into practice. At times the attempt to do so has been ineffective; at other times it has been destructive. If theology cannot be effectively implemented through institutional structures, something is clearly wrong with either the theology or the polity or both.

Methodists have been a practical people. Their emphasis has been on bringing persons to an understanding of the grace of God. Methodism began as a revival movement that had a profound impact on the larger society. It witnessed to people who wanted to be saved from their sins and to flee from the wrath to come. Its theology was and continues to be tested in the reality of carrying forth its mission in the world.

For two centuries Methodist leaders from across the connection have assembled in conference to review where they are, to plan for the coming quadrennium, and to update the bylaws under which the denomination will operate. Every four years *The Discipline* is revised, a practice that reflects the church's attempt to be as effective as possible in a constantly changing context.

The Discipline of today is considerably different from that of a generation or two earlier. With the exception of a few sections such as the Articles of Religion and certain historic features, the current version would be almost unrecognizable when compared to the edition seventy-five or a hundred years ago. The world of the twentieth century is far removed from that of the nineteenth and even further removed from that of the eighteenth. It is safe to assume that the twenty-first century will be greatly different from the present. The continuing interaction between theology and polity helps keep Methodism's faith and practice relevant to a dynamic context. The words of the Charles Wesley hymn states what the task of the church continues to be: "To serve the present age, my calling to fulfill. . . ."

Like other Christians, United Methodists are a pilgrim people whose particular doctrinal heritage, theological understandings, and institutional structures contribute to their mission in the world. The church has stated its goal to be "the continually renewed grasp of the gospel of God's love in Christ and its application to the ceaseless crises of human existence."[2] Churches throughout Christian history have organized themselves in a variety of ways. The task for every generation is to be sure that their witness is faithful and the institutional structures effective in communicating the gospel and carrying out the mission of the church in their age.

NOTES

1. Jerry L. Walls, *The Problem of Pluralism* (Wilmore, Ky.: Good News Books, 1986), is an example of a serious and substantive wrestling with this issue.

2. *The Book of Discipline of The United Methodist Church, 1984* (Nashville: United Methodist Publishing House, 1984), para. 69.

Suggestions for Further Reading

There are literally hundreds of books on Methodist theology and polity. The following list contains some recent and readily available works on these subjects. They will prove useful to anyone wishing to probe more deeply into the relationship between United Methodist theology and polity.

Duecker, R. Sheldon. *Tensions in the Connection: Issues Facing United Methodism.* Nashville: Abingdon Press, 1983. 128 pages.

A discussion of current issues including the itineracy, the decision-making process, clergy evaluation, and leadership of the United Methodist Church.

Harmon, Nolan B. *Understanding the United Methodist Church,* revised ed. Nashville: Abingdon Press, 1977. 176 pages.

The book that for two decades was the basic guide to the doctrines and discipline of Methodism.

Harper, Steve. *John Wesley's Message for Today.* Grand Rapids: Zondervan, Francis Asbury Press, 1983. 146 pages.

A presentation of the major doctrinal emphases of John Wesley with their relevance for the contemporary Christian.

Johnson, Douglas W., and Alan K. Waltz. *Facts and Possibilities: An Agenda for the United Methodist Church.* Nashville: Abingdon Press, 1987. 157 pages.

An account of how recent mergers and other denominational decisions have influenced United Methodism.

Langford, Thomas A. *Practical Divinity: Theology in the Wesleyan Spirit.* Nashville: Abingdon Press, 1983. 303 pages.

A valuable survey of Methodist theology in both Britain and America from John Wesley to the present.

———. *Wesleyan Theology: A Sourcebook.* Durham, N.C.: Labyrinth Press, 1984. 309 pages.

Selections from the writings of Methodist theologians from John Wesley to the present.

Matthews, James K. *Set Apart to Serve: The Role of the Episcopacy in the Wesleyan Tradition.* Nashville: Abingdon Press, 1985. 331 pages.

A history of the development of the episcopacy and the current role and function of the bishop in the United Methodist Church.

Mickey, Paul A., and Robert L. Wilson. *What New Creation? The Agony of Church Restructure.* Nashville: Abingdon Press, 1977. 192 pages.

The nature of the national church bureaucracy, how it functions, its theological foundations, and its direction for the future.

Norwood, Frederick A. *The Story of American Methodism.* Nashville: Abingdon Press, 1974. 447 pages.

A history of Methodism in America from its beginning to the present. The development of the Evangelical Association and the United Brethren is included.

Sherwood, John R., and John C. Wagner. *Sources and Shapes of Power.* Nashville: Abingdon Press, 1981. 125 pages.

A book that explores the nature of leadership of the United Methodist Church with particular emphasis on the annual conference.

Short, Roy H. *United Methodism in Theory and Practice.* Nashville: Abingdon Press, 1974. 205 pages.

An analysis of United Methodist concepts and practices, including connectionalism, the ministry, the episcopacy, and the conference system.

Tuell, Jack M. *The Organization of the United Methodist Church*, revised ed. Nashville: Abingdon Press, 1985. 173 pages.

A summary volume on how the United Methodist Church is organized. This book is useful as a companion to *The Discipline*.

Walls, Jerry L. *The Problem of Pluralism: Recovering United Methodist Identity*. Wilmore, Ky.: Good News Books, 1986. 141 pages.

A discussion of the nature and problems related to pluralism, which the United Methodist Church now affirms as a principle.

Waltz, Alan K. *To Proclaim the Faith*. Nashville: Abingdon Press, 1983. 142 pages.

A book that gives a historical summary of how Methodist people put their faith in action and explores the church's potential for the future.

Wilson, Robert L. *Shaping the Congregation*. Nashville: Abingdon Press, 1981. 128 pages.

How the social forces operating within the community, the local church, and the denomination influence the nature and the functioning of the congregation.

Index of Persons

The designation *n* after a page number indicates an endnote.

Index of Subjects

The designation *n* after a page number indicates an endnote.

Index of Subjects